The
Victoria Cross
and
George Cross
Collection of

THIS
HALL OF VALOUR
COMMEMORATING
THE HEROISM AND SACRIFICES OF AUSTRALIANS
WAS OPENED BY
HIS ROYAL HIGHNESS THE PRINCE OF WALES
ON 15 APRIL 1981

THEY DARED
MIGHTILY

THEY DARED MIGHTILY

Lionel Wigmore
in collaboration with
Bruce Harding

Second edition
revised and condensed
by
Jeff Williams
and
Anthony Staunton

AUSTRALIAN WAR MEMORIAL
CANBERRA

First published in 1986 by
the Australian War Memorial
Canberra ACT 2600

© Australian War Memorial 1986

Designed and produced by
John Ferguson Pty Ltd
133 Macquarie Street
Sydney NSW 2000

National Library of Australia
Cataloguing-in-publication data

Wigmore, Lionel.
They dared mightily.

2nd ed.
Includes index.
ISBN 0 642 99471 4.

1. Victoria Cross. 2. George Medal. 3. Australia — Armed
Forces — Medals, badges, decorations, etc. 4. Australia —
Armed Forces — Biography. I. Harding, Bruce A. (Bruce
Alfred), 1920- . II. Williams, Jeffrey, 1954- .
III. Staunton, Anthony, 1948- . IV. Australian War
Memorial. V. Title.

355.1'342'0922

Printed in Singapore

Front cover painting by Geoffrey Mainwaring
Australians in action at Buna 1962 (detail)
oil on canvas
Australian War Memorial (27547)

The pictures used to open each new section are taken
from the Australian War Memorial's archives and have
the following file numbers: South Africa 1899–1902 AWM 4948,
The 1914–18 war AWM 2022, North Russia 1919 AWM 4894,
The 1939–45 war AWM 17361, Vietnam 1962–72 AWM CUN/66/194/VN.

CONTENTS

PREFACE

The original 1963 edition of this standard reference work has become something of a classic of Australian military history. However, the years since its publication have brought not only four new Victoria Cross winners from among the Australians who served in Vietnam, but also much new research into the lives and circumstances of many of the earlier recipients. When the volume went out of print, therefore, the Australian War Memorial decided that a completely new and revised edition should be prepared that would incorporate all this new information. At the same time, all the entries were condensed, and the official citations were deleted in favour of retaining the most accurate and up-to-date possible account of the actions for which the awards were won.

ACKNOWLEDGEMENTS

We wish to acknowledge with gratitude and warmth the assistance of many people. Especial thanks are due to the staff who maintain the meticulous records of the Australian Dictionary of Biography. In revising the excellent work of the original writers of this book, we accepted the considerable help offered by Dr Chris Cunneen, Merrilyn Lincoln and Jim Gibbney.

Dr Michael McKernan, the Assistant Director (Research and Publications) at the Memorial, initiated the revised edition. We are grateful for his energy and encouragement, and for the support given by his very able research and publications staff, Megan Cook, Peter Stanley, Margaret Browne and Matthew Higgins. Helpful and enthusiastic assistance can always be found in the Memorial's Research Centre. Contributors from this area were Geoff McKeown, Michael Piggott, Ron Gilchrist and Steve Corvini.

Individuals deserving special thanks are Canon William M. Lummis, MC, Dennis Pillinger, Bob Mansell, Rose Coombs, John Winton, F.G. Birks, Janet Shaw, Judith McClymont, John Price, Ken White, Warren Perry, Greg Doolan, Ray Tancred, Steve Penny, Des and Christina Burke, Ken Cox and Bob Connell.

Appreciation and acknowledgement are due also to the Central Army Records Office, Melbourne; the Australian War Graves Commission; the National Library of Australia; and the State Library of Victoria.

Undoubtedly the best source for background to the institution of the award of the Victoria Cross is the monumental work of M.J. Crook, *The Evolution of the Victoria Cross* (Tunbridge Wells, 1975).

Jeff Williams
Anthony Staunton

ABBREVIATIONS

AAMC	Australian Army Medical Corps
AASC	Australian Army Service Corps
AATTV	Australian Army Training Team, Vietnam
AFC	Australian Flying Corps
AIF	Australian Imperial Force
ALP	Australian Labor Party
AMF	Australian Military Forces
CBE	Commander of the Order of the British Empire
CIDG	Civilian Irregular Defence Group
CMF	Citizen Military Forces
CMG	Companion of the Order of St Michael and St George
DCM	Distinguished Conduct Medal
FRCS	Fellow of the Royal College of Surgeons
HMAT	His Majesty's Australian Transport
KCB	Knight Commander of the Bath
KCMG	Knight Commander of the Order of St Michael and St George
LRCP	Licentiate of the Royal College of Physicians
MC	Military Cross
MHR	Member of the House of Representatives
MM	Military Medal
MP	Member of Parliament
MRCS	Member of the Royal College of Surgeons
MSM	Meritorious Service Medal
OBE	Officer, Order of the British Empire
RAAF	Royal Australian Air Force
RAF	Royal Air Force
RAMC	Royal Army Medical Corps
RFC	Royal Flying Corps
RSL	Returned Services League of Australia
SEATO	South-East Asian Treaty Organization

INTRODUCTION: THE VICTORIA CROSS

IN 1856 Queen Victoria signed the first warrant instituting the Victoria Cross. The warrant consisted of a preamble in which the need for such a decoration was explained. There followed a description of the cross, together with fifteen rules and ordinances covering its award. The Victoria Cross was to be 'a new Naval and Military decoration, which we are desirous should be highly prized and eagerly sought after by Officers and Men of Our Naval and Military Service'. Clause five stated that 'the cross would only be awarded to those officers and men who have served Us in the presence of the enemy and shall then have performed some signal act of valour or devotion to their country'. The next clause added 'that neither rank nor long service nor wounds nor any other circumstance or condition whatsoever save the merit of conspicuous bravery shall be held to establish a sufficient claim for the honour'. The distinction is highly prized and has evolved into the supreme decoration for gallantry in battle awarded to members of Commonwealth forces in the last 130 years.

In 1854, Britain, which had not fought a major war since its victory at Waterloo in 1815, became involved in a war with Russia. A number of defects were quickly evident in the leadership and administration of the army. These were emphasized by the charge of the Light Brigade and the need for Florence Nightingale's work in the army hospitals. Another deficiency was the lack of any appropriate recognition for gallantry. Several means of recognition existed but each had its shortcomings. Mentions in dispatches were indiscriminate and in many cases all officers above a certain rank were cited. Brevet promotions were similarly indiscriminate and often went to staff officers rather than those company officers more directly involved in the fighting. The need for a new decoration was particularly evident because newspapers, for the first time, were making the public more aware of the deeds of the ordinary soldier.

The credit for first bringing these arguments to the attention of the public should go to Captain G.T. Scholl, MP. On 18 December 1854 he moved in the House of Commons that an Order of Merit should be instituted to recognize distinguished and prominent personal gallantry of members of the army and navy then fighting in the Crimea. Having debated the matter in the Commons and having been assured that the question was under consideration, he withdrew his motion. As a direct result of this debate, the Secretary of War, the Duke of Newcastle, wrote to Albert, the Prince Consort, on 20 January 1854.

Albert replied two days later and supported the proposal that a new decoration be instituted. He also suggested how the new award should be implemented. The Duke of Newcastle announced to the House of Lords a week later that a Cross of Merit, open to all ranks, would shortly be introduced. A year later this Cross of Merit would evolve into the Victoria Cross.

The first recipient was Lieutenant Charles Lucas of HMS *Hecla* for gallantry in the Baltic on 21 June 1854. Lucas threw overboard a live shell during an attack on the shore batteries at Bomarsund. The first awards to the army were made to six officers and men for gallantry during the battle of Alma in the Crimea on 20 September 1854. The first flying Victoria Cross was made to Second Lieutenant William Rhodes-Moorhouse posthumously in 1915. His mother had been born in New Zealand and was part Maori. His son was killed in action twenty-five years later during the Battle of Britain and his ashes were interred next to his father.

The warrant signed by Queen Victoria was made retrospective to the autumn of 1854. Eventually 111 awards were made for acts of valour

in the Crimean war. The first ceremonial presentation of the Victoria Cross took place in Hyde Park, London, on 26 June 1857, when the Queen invested sixty-two recipients before a crowd of over 100 000. Queen Victoria, dressed in field marshal's uniform, was accompanied by Albert, the Prince Consort. She presented the new award firstly to twelve members of the Royal Navy, followed by two Royal Marines and then forty-eight members of the army. The first presentation in Australia was made to Private Frederick Whirlpool of the Hawthorn and East Kew Rifles who won the award as a member of the 3rd Bombay European Fusiliers at Jhansi on 2 May 1858 during the Indian mutiny. He received his cross from Sir Henry Barkly, KCB, the governor of Victoria, at Albert Park, Melbourne, on 20 June 1861. He lived in Australia until his death at Windsor, NSW, on 24 June 1898 where he is buried in an unmarked grave. At the time of writing his medals have been loaned to the Australian War Memorial for display.

The conditions of award outlined in Queen Victoria's original warrant of 1856 have been extended several times to suit altered circumstances. Initially the Victoria Cross was instituted for award to the 'Officers and Men of Our Naval and Military Services' and colonial soldiers were therefore not eligible. During the Maori wars, however, on 11 February 1864, Charles Heaphy, a captain in the Auckland City Volunteers, performed an act of valour for which he was recommended for the Victoria

Cross.

The New Zealand governor, Sir George Grey, was informed by the British government that the recommendation could not be entertained because of the limitations of the original warrant. The two governments debated the issue for the next two years in their correspondence until, as a direct result of Heaphy's case, Queen Victoria signed a Royal Warrant on 1 January 1867 which extended the original and now covered 'Local Forces raised, or which may be raised, in Our Colonies and their dependencies... for the suppression of rebellion against Our authority, or for repelling invasion by a Foreign enemy'. Heaphy received the Victoria Cross in February 1867 and colonial soldiers from that time on were placed on equal footing with members of the British regular forces. Heaphy is also remembered as an artist and explorer. He was judge of the Native Land Court in New Zealand until ill health caused his resignation in June 1881. He sailed for Australia where he died in Brisbane on 3 August 1881 and was buried in Toowong cemetery.

Since the creation of the Victoria Cross, 1354 crosses have been awarded, the latest recipients being Colonel Herbert Jones and Sergeant Ian McKay of the 2nd Parachute Regiment for their actions during fighting for the Falklands in 1982. Three men have received the Victoria Cross twice, including Captain Charles Hazlitt Upham of New Zealand during the 1939–45 war. In three instances it has been awarded to father and son; on four occasions awards have been made to brothers; awards have been made to five civilians serving under military command. Six Victoria Crosses have been awarded for bravery not in the face of the enemy. The conditions for the award were widened in 1858 to cover situations which would now earn the award of the George Cross. In 1881, the warrant was rewritten and the original concept of only bravery in the face of the enemy was restored. The first of these six awards was to Timothy O'Hea. Born in 1846 at Bantry, Ireland, O'Hea went to Canada as a member of the Rifle Brigade. At Danville, near Quebec, on 8 June 1866, he distinguished himself by quelling, at great risk, a fire on an ammunition train to which were attached carriages containing about 200 German migrants. He was presented with the Victoria Cross at Quebec in April 1867 and left the army shortly afterwards. O'Hea travelled to New Zealand where he served in the police force. In June 1874 he arrived in Sydney where Eccleston Du Faur was financing Andrew Hume's search for a supposed survivor of the 1848 Leichhardt expedition. O'Hea joined Hume and a third man, Lewis Thompson, and went into south-western Queensland in November 1874. The result was almost a repetition of the Burke and Wills tragedy as Hume and O'Hea died of thirst about 80 kilometres west of the Wilson River, leaving Thompson to stagger back to Nockatunga station. O'Hea's body was never found. His Victoria Cross was subsequently presented to the Art Gallery of New

South Wales, who presented it to the Rifle Brigade in 1951 and it is now on display in the museum of the Royal Green Jackets at Winchester.

All of the Victoria Crosses presented so far have been manufactured from gun metal taken from Russian artillery pieces captured during the Crimean war. Initially Victoria Crosses were fashioned from small ingots which were smelted from the cascabel plugs of two Russian bronze smooth-bore muzzle-loading guns. During the 1939–45 war the remaining stock of metal was destroyed by enemy air action so the cascabel plug was cut from another Russian gun captured at Sebastapol. This metal, stored in the Equipments Sub-Depot of the Royal Army Ordnance Corps Central Depot at Donnington, Shropshire, is officially described as 9680–99–964–0816 V.C. Gunmetal.

Since 1857, when Lord Panmure, Secretary of State for War, entrusted the work to them, all crosses have been made by Hancocks and Company (Jewellers) Ltd, now of Vigo Street, London. Hancocks, who hold a small stock of gun metal on behalf of the three services, sand-cast six crosses at a time. The hardness of the metal necessitates casting at a temperature of 2000°F as no other process, such as pressing with dies, is satisfactory. The temperature of the molten bronze is critical — if it is too hot the mould will be damaged and if too cold the metal will not flow evenly. The bar, decorated with laurel leaves and bearing a 'V' from which the cross hangs, is cast separately.

After casting, the crosses are cleared and then passed to the 'chaser' who brings the lettering into sharp relief, engraves minute detail and adds the maker's secret mark to guard against forgeries. The crosses are then bronzed to a uniform colour and sent to the War Office for approval. Only the engraving of the recipients' particulars — rank, name and date or dates of the action being honoured — remains to be done and Hancocks carry this out as required from their stock of crosses.

There is some controversy as to the actual number of Australians who have been awarded the Victoria Cross. This book outlines the exploits and biographies of ninety-six winners of the Victoria Cross: it spans the period from the award to Captain Neville Howse of the NSW Army Medical Corps on 24 July 1900 during the South African war, to that made to Warrant Officer II Keith Payne of the Australian Army Training Team on 24 May 1969, in Vietnam. It includes those Victoria Cross winners who had served in Australia's armed forces, either before or at the time of their award, or who had lived in Australia for a significant period before receiving the Victoria Cross. A number of Victoria Cross winners have become associated with Australia, through migrating to Australia after winning the award as members of other nation's forces or by other connections. Sixteen other Victoria Cross winners have lived in Australia, some for up to forty years, and sixteen are buried here. Appendix I gives brief biographical details of Victoria Cross winners who were born in or who have died in Australia and who are not included with the main ninety-six biographies.

Ninety-one members of Australian forces have won the Victoria Cross and all have full biographies in this book. Five winners who received their Victoria Cross while serving with British forces, and in one case the South African Constabulary, are also given full biographies. These five, prior to winning the Victoria Cross, had served with Australian military forces and were, with the exception of Samuel Pearse, all born in Australia.

Various claims have been made for the identification as 'Australian VCs' beyond the ninety-six individuals accorded full entries in this book. It is true, for example, that Lieutenant Colonel Mark Sever Bell was the first person born in Australia to receive the Victoria Cross. Bell was born in Sydney in 1843 of British parents and left Australia as an infant. He became an officer of the British Royal Engineers and was awarded the Victoria Cross for an act of bravery at the battle of Ordashu during the Ashante war of 1874. Bell, however, never returned to Australia and can therefore hardly be regarded as an Australian.

Lieutenant George Moor was born of British parents in Melbourne in 1896 but like Bell left Australia as a child. He won the Victoria Cross while attached to the 2nd Battalion of the Hampshire Regiment at Krithia, Gallipoli, in June 1915.

Soldiers dominate the awards. Ninety-three Victoria Cross holders were members of army units and the remaining three were members of air force units. Of the army awards one, that to Lieutenant F.H. McNamara of No. 1 Squadron, Australian Flying Corps, AIF, was made when he, flying a bi-plane, rescued a fellow pilot from behind enemy lines. As mentioned earlier, Edwards and Middleton were either serving with or attached to RAF units when they were awarded their crosses. The remaining Australian air force recipient was Flight Lieutenant Bill Newton of No. 22 Squadron, RAAF, for actions on Salamaua Isthmus, New Guinea, on 16–17 March 1943. No Victoria Cross has been awarded to a member of the Royal Australian Navy, although members of naval forces are specifically stated to be eligible. It is noteworthy, however, that of Australians awarded the George Cross, four were members of the Royal Australian Naval Volunteer Reserve and another of the Royal Australian Navy. (The George Cross is treated in Appendix II and its winners, as well as those who converted other awards to George Crosses, are listed there.)

Although the instituting warrant made no reference to posthumous awards, it had been decided from the very beginning that the cross would not be given for an act in which the potential recipient was killed. In such cases it was announced in the *London Gazette* that had the person concerned survived he would have been recommended for the Victoria Cross. During the South African war, 1898–1902, six posthumous awards were gazetted but the policy against posthumous awards remained unchanged because of the six earlier cases where the notice in the *London Gazette* stated that they would have been recommended had they survived. In late 1906, a petition from the widow of one of these men moved King Edward VII to send the cross to their next-of-kin. In two cases it was for acts of bravery performed nearly fifty years before in the Indian mutiny. With the transmission of the Victoria Cross to the relatives of these men, and with the precedent set in the South African war, there was no further objection to posthumous awards. Over 180 posthumous awards were made in the 1914–18 war although specific provision for posthumous awards was only written into the consolidating Royal Warrant of 22 May 1920. Twenty-eight Australians have been awarded the Victoria Cross posthumously — fifteen during the 1914–18 war, one in north Russia, ten in the 1939–45 war, and two in Vietnam.

The Victoria Cross comes first in the order of precedence of British and Commonwealth awards and the winner is entitled to the post-nominals 'VC'. When the ribbon alone is worn a miniature replica of the Victoria Cross is borne on its centre; a bar to the medal is shown by wearing an additional miniature cross. On 1 June 1951 it was announced that military funerals were to be accorded to all Victoria Cross winners who die in Australia. The Australian War Graves Commission maintains in perpetuity the graves of Victoria Cross winners and in 1983 restored the graves of two British Army Victoria Cross winners

who had died at the turn of the century and whose graves in the Melbourne (Carlton) cemetery were somewhat neglected. In 1980 the then Prime Minister, Mr J.M. Fraser, granted free travel for up to six flights a year with domestic airlines for Victoria Cross and George Cross winners.

His Royal Highness, Charles, the Prince of Wales, opened a new gallery, the Hall of Valour, at the Australian War Memorial on 13 April 1981. This gallery replaced 'Victoria Cross Corner', opened in November 1964, which had accommodated the Memorial's collection of six crosses. The collection has expanded rapidly: there are now thirty-six Victoria Crosses in one of the largest collections in the world. Also represented in the hall are men and women who were highly decorated in other ways. Included in the present collection are the first cross awarded to an Australian serviceman; five of the seven Victoria Crosses awarded for actions at Lone Pine on Gallipoli; one of the two Victoria Crosses awarded for service in North Russia in 1919; the first cross awarded to an Australian as well as the three Victoria Crosses awarded to Australian airmen in the 1939–45 war; and two of the four crosses awarded for service in Vietnam.

In addition to the Hall of Valour, there are many other memorials to Victoria Cross winners in Australia. Victoria Crosses won by Australians are on display in museums or other public places in all states of Australia. Many streets have been named after Victoria Cross winners, particularly in Canberra, where over sixty streets have been named in their honour. The suburb of Gowrie in Canberra is named for a governor-general of Australia who won the Victoria Cross with the British Army. The names of Victoria Cross winners appear on some individual war memorials as well as on local town and city war memorials. Many soldiers' clubs are named for Victoria Cross winners. Perhaps the most unusual memorial is the town of Holbrook in New South Wales which was renamed after a Royal Navy Victoria Cross winner. In the 1914–18 war, many towns with German names changed them because of the war and although some changed back when peace came, others, including Holbrook, retained their new names. Commander Holbrook, VC, was greatly honoured by the naming and visited the town a number of times prior to his death in 1975. His widow returned to Holbrook in May 1982 and presented his Victoria Cross and other medals to the town where they are now displayed.

The following entries tell of the deeds which earned Australians or members of Australian units Britain's highest and most coveted decoration for bravery. Each award is dealt with separately and the specific deed as well as a brief account of the campaign and the particular action to which it relates are given. A biographical background and an account of each recipient's subsequent career are also included.

South Africa 1899–1902

BELL Frederick William

RANK   Lieutenant
UNIT   6th West Australian
            Mounted Infantry
DATE   16 May 1901
PLACE   Brakpan, Transvaal

F.W. BELL, born on 3 April 1875 in Perth, Western Australia, son of Henry and Agnes Bell, was educated at A.D. Letch's preparatory school and at the government school, Perth. He joined the Western Australian Public Service in 1894 as a cadet in the Department of Customs where he later became a cashier.

In October 1899 he enlisted in the 1st West Australian (Mounted Infantry) Contingent raised by Western Australia for service in South Africa. He arrived in South Africa on 27 November and saw action at Slingersfontein and later took part in the relief of Johannesburg and Pretoria and the battles of Diamond Hill and Wittebergen. On 19 July 1900 he was seriously wounded in an engagement with Boers at Palmeitfontein and was invalided to Britain. Bell returned to Western Australia in February 1901 and settled at Cottesloe. He was commissioned lieutenant in the 6th Contingent on 8 March, and re-embarked for South Africa. The 6th Contingent, for most of its term in South Africa, was attached to Kitchener's column which conducted several large sweeps through the eastern Transvaal and the Orange Free State. During one of these operations Bell performed the act for which he was awarded the Victoria Cross.

On 16 May at Brakpan, Transvaal, while his unit was retiring through a heavy fire, Bell returned to pick up a dismounted man and took him up on his horse. The animal fell under the additional weight and Bell, after insisting that the man take the horse, covered him until he was out of danger.

After his discharge in May 1902, Bell joined the Australian section of the coronation escort for King Edward VII. On 1 July, the Prince of Wales inspected the colonial contingents at the Horse Guards and presented the Victoria Cross to Farrier-Major Hardham of New Zealand, Bell and to two South Africans. Because the parade had been quickly arranged the Victoria Cross had not been engraved before the presentation and was returned after the ceremony for Bell's name and details to be engraved. He settled in Perth but returned to Britain where he joined the colonial service in 1905. He went to British Somaliland as an assistant district officer in April. In late 1905 Bell was made an assistant political officer and he held the post until 1910. During this period he took up big game hunting (specializing in lion-hunting), and in 1909 was severely mauled by a lion. From 1910 until 1912 he was assistant resident in Nigeria and from then until the outbreak of the 1914–18 war was an assistant district commissioner in Kenya.

During this war Bell served as an officer in the British army. He went to France with the Royal Irish Dragoon Guards, was mentioned in dispatches and promoted to captain in October 1915. On his return to Britain he was made commandant of a rest camp and promoted to major. Later, as a lieutenant colonel, he commanded an embarkation camp at Plymouth. Two of his three brothers were killed in action with the AIF, Edgar at Gallipoli and Bert at Pozières.

After the war Bell returned to Kenya as a district commissioner. In May 1922 he married Mabel Valentini and in 1925 retired in Britain. His wife died in 1944 and he married Brenda Cracklow who survived him when he died at Bristol on 28 April 1954.

BISDEE John Hutton

RANK Trooper
UNIT 1st Tasmanian Imperial Bushmen
DATE 1 September 1900
PLACE Warm Bad, Transvaal

JOHN BISDEE, the eighth child of John and Ellen Jane Bisdee, was born on 28 September 1869 at Hutton Park, Melton Mowbray, Tasmania. His grandfather, John Bisdee, had arrived in the colony in 1821. He was educated at The Hutchins School, Hobart, and then worked on his father's property until April 1900 when he enlisted for service in the South African war as a trooper in the 1st Tasmanian Imperial Bushmen.

Bisdee sailed on 26 April and served in operations in the Orange River Colony and the Transvaal. On 1 September, near Warm Bad, Bisdee and other members of an advance scouting party were ambushed by Boers in a rocky defile. Six of the party of eight were hit including the two officers, Major Brooke and Lieutenant Wylly [q.v.]. Brooke's horse had bolted so Bisdee dismounted, put the officer on his own horse and ran alongside, then mounted behind him and withdrew under heavy fire. For this he received the Victoria Cross, the first gazetted to an Australian-born soldier serving in an Australian unit.

Wounded during the ambush, Bisdee was invalided home but on recovering returned to South Africa as a lieutenant in No. 1 Company, 2nd Tasmanian Imperial Bushmen, and served from March 1901 until the end of the war.

He returned to Tasmania and resumed mixed farming at Hutton Park. On 11 April 1904 he married Georgiana Theodosia Hale, daughter of Bishop Hale. In 1906 he joined the 12th Australian Light Horse Regiment, Tasmanian Mounted Infantry, as a temporary lieutenant and had been promoted to captain by 1910, the same year in which he attended a course of instruction in India. In August 1913 he became commanding officer of the 26th Light Horse.

Bisdee joined the AIF on 26 July 1915 and was allotted to the 12th Light Horse. In November–December he was with the Australian Composite Regiment operating against the Senussi in Egypt until he was wounded in the leg. He was seconded as assistant provost marshal, AIF Headquarters, Egypt, in March 1916, then to the Anzac Mounted Division. Promoted to major in September, he served with the 12th Light Horse throughout 1917. In January 1918 he became assistant provost marshal (Egypt) of the Anzac Provost Corps and in June was confirmed as lieutenant colonel. He was mentioned in dispatches and appointed OBE in June 1919.

Bisdee was discharged from the AIF in May 1920, placed on the reserve list in 1921 and on the retired list in 1929. He had continued to farm on his property at Ashburton, Bridgewater, in Tasmania, the property he had acquired in 1915. While travelling in France in 1926 his wife died. He returned to Tranquility, Melton Mowbray, Tasmania, where he died of chronic nephritis on 14 January 1930; he was buried in St James's churchyard, Jericho, in the same grave as his sister.

The Bisdee Memorial Cadet Efficiency Prize, awarded annually at St Virgil's College, Hobart, is named after him. His Victoria Cross is displayed in the Tasmanian Museum and Art Gallery, Hobart.

HOWSE Neville Reginald

RANK   Captain
UNIT   New South Wales
          Army Medical Corps
DATE   24 July 1900
PLACE   Vredefort, Orange Free
          State

NEVILLE HOWSE was born on 26 October 1863 in Stogursey, Somerset, UK. The second son of Alfred and Lucy Elizabeth Howse, he was educated at Fullard's House School, Taunton. He entered London Hospital as a student in 1882 and gained the diplomas of MRCS and LRCP in 1886. He emigrated to Australia in 1889 and set up practice at Taree, New South Wales, but in 1895 returned to Britain to undertake postgraduate study and two years later became an FRCS. He returned to Australia in 1899 and practised in Orange, New South Wales, prior to his departure for South Africa as a lieutenant in the second contingent of the New South Wales Medical Corps a few months later. The contingent arrived in South Africa on 22 February 1900.

In July 1900 elements of the Medical Corps were attached to a mounted infantry brigade, commanded by Brigadier General C.P. Ridley, which was in pursuit of an enemy force led by the Boer general, Christiaan de Wet. On the 24th de Wet's forces clashed with the mounted infantry near a Boer farm named Stinkhoutboom near Vredefort. Two guns were brought up and fired from hidden positions. At the height of the fighting Howse saw a trumpeter fall wounded in the foremost line. Howse galloped out under extremely heavy fire to rescue the man. Howse's horse was shot dead, but he continued on foot to the casualty, treated his wounds and carried him out of the action. His Victoria Cross was the first awarded to an Australian soldier and is still the only one to have been received by a medical member of the Australian forces. Howse was promoted to captain in October 1900.

Promoted to honorary major, he returned to South Africa in command of the bearer company of the Australian medical contingent. The contingent left Sydney in February 1902, saw service with a mounted infantry column and returned to Australia in August. On 4 December he was decorated with his Victoria Cross at Victoria Barracks, Paddington, and among the first two to congratulate him were Victoria Cross winners of the Indian mutiny, Alfred Heathcote and John Paton, who had been resident in New South Wales for many years. The *Sydney Mail* report of the presentation stated that, shortly after winning the Victoria Cross, Howse had attended a Queensland officer under fire and was taken prisoner by the Boers but released six weeks later as a noncombatant. On his return from South Africa he resumed his practice in Orange and was its mayor when war broke out in August 1914.

He joined the Australian Naval and Military Expeditionary Force as principal medical officer and went with that force to seize German New Guinea in September 1914. Howse returned from New Guinea just in time to obtain leave to sail with the 1st Division as supernumerary medical officer. As Assistant Director Medical Services in Major General Bridges's 1st Australian Division, he landed at Gallipoli on 25 April 1915. Here he gave outstanding service in personally attending the wounded and formulating medical arrangements for which he was mentioned in dispatches and created a Companion of the Order of the Bath. He became Deputy Director Medical Services ANZAC on 11 September 1915. During the latter months of 1915 the structure of Australian medical services was debated between Australia and the British War Office. As a result, Howse was appointed in charge on a temporary basis and given the rank of surgeon general. He was soon confirmed as Director of Medical Services, AIF, and remained as administrative head of AIF Medical Services until after the war ended. From 1917 until near the end of the war, a major issue developed between the AIF and Australia on the enlistment and military employment of men below the physical standard. The issue was not clinical but political, particularly in the light of falling recruitment and the failure of the conscription referenda. Howse steadfastly refused to support a policy of dilution by the lowering of physical standards. C.E.W. Bean wrote that 'Unquestionably the AIF also owed its physique and morale partly to the will and ability of Surgeon-General Howse'.

At the end of 1918, Howse returned to Australia on Anzac leave and also to advise the Minister for Defence on issues relating to AIF medical services. He arrived in Sydney on Armistice Day and after a short leave he returned to Britain in February 1919 to supervise the medical aspects of the large-scale repatriation programme. His AIF appointment ended on 1 January 1920.

In January 1917 Howse was created Knight Commander of the Bath; in 1919 he became KCMG and a Knight of Grace of the Order of St John of Jerusalem. In July 1921 he was appointed Director General Medical Services (DGMS) in the AMF. Howse resigned in 1922 and was elected to the House of Representatives for the seat of Calare, which included Orange, as a member of the National Party. He was reappointed DGMS on a part-time basis until he entered the Cabinet in 1925. He had been appointed temporary Chairman of Committees in 1923 and 1924, and the following year he became minister for the portfolios of defence and health in the Bruce–Page government (16 January 1925 to 2 April 1927). He was later honorary minister (2 April 1927 to 24 February 1928), Minister for Home and Territories (24 February 1928 to 29 November 1928) and Minister for Health (16 January 1925 to 2 April 1927 and 24 February 1928 to 22 October 1929). He lost his seat in the 1929 election, sailed for Britain in February 1930 and died of cancer in London on 19 September. He was buried at Kensal Green cemetery.

Sir Neville had married Evelyn Gertrude Northcote Pilcher at Bathurst in 1905. He was survived by his wife, two sons and three daughters. In 1931 a memorial plaque to him was unveiled in the Soldiers' Memorial Hall at Orange. A commemorative plaque has been erected in the Australian Institute of Anatomy.

All of Howse's medals and decorations are on display in the Australian War Memorial's Hall of Valour, as is a portrait of him by James Quinn. In the headquarters of the RAMC in London there is a painting by Sir William Dargie which depicts Howse winning the Victoria Cross.

MAYGAR Leslie Cecil

RANK Lieutenant
UNIT 5th Victorian Mounted Rifles
DATE 23 November 1901
PLACE Geelhoutboom, Natal

L.C. MAYGAR was born on 26 May 1872 at Dean Station, Kilmore, Victoria, to Edwin Willis and Helen Maygar. He was educated at Kilmore and Alexandria state schools, then worked on his father's property. Later, with his father and brother, he became a partner in the firm of H. Maygar & Sons, owners of Strathearn Estate, Euroa, Victoria. He enlisted in the Victorian Mounted Rifles in March 1891. Although Maygar attempted several times to enlist for active service with the first and subsequent contingents of the Rifles which left for South Africa, physical disabilities prevented him doing so until his acceptance into the fifth contingent; he had been promoted to lieutenant. The fifth arrived in

South Africa in March 1901 and joined General Beatson's column in which they saw much action. In August they transferred to Natal, as part of a column commanded by Colonel Pulteney, to assist in actions against General Louis Botha, and in this sector the Victorians were constantly in action against strong commando forces. This arduous service continued until March 1902 when the contingent was withdrawn for return to Australia.

It was at Geelhoutboom on 23 November 1901 that Maygar won his Victoria Cross. He galloped out to a detached post which was being outflanked, and ordered the men to retire. The horse of Saddler A. Short, also a Victorian, was shot from under him and Maygar dismounted and lifted Short on to his own horse. The horse bolted into boggy ground and both men had to dismount. Maygar, realizing that the horse could only carry one person, ordered Short to gallop for cover. Maygar followed on foot, evading the heavy rifle fire around him. He was also mentioned in dispatches for his service in South Africa. On 8 June 1902 a large ceremonial parade was held in Pretoria to celebrate the end of the war and Kitchener presented the Victoria Cross to Maygar.

Maygar returned to Australia in 1902, carried his commission into the 8th Light Horse Regiment and was promoted to captain on 9 May 1905. In July 1912 he transferred to the 16th (Indi) Light Horse Regiment. When the 1914–18 war broke out Maygar quickly volunteered for service and was a member of the advance party which laid out the first light horse camp at Broadmeadows, Victoria. On 20 August 1914 he was appointed captain in the AIF and posted as officer commanding B Squadron, 4th Light Horse Regiment, with which he sailed for Egypt in October.

During service on Gallipoli Maygar was promoted to major and on 17 October 1915 succeeded to the command of the 8th Light Horse Regiment, with the temporary rank of lieutenant colonel. His rank and appointment were confirmed in December and Maygar led the 8th throughout its service in Sinai and Palestine. On three occasions in 1917 Maygar temporarily commanded the 3rd Light Horse Brigade. In October 1917 he was awarded the Distinguished Service Order for distinguished service in the field. He was mentioned in dispatches in December 1916, July 1917 and January 1918 and qualified for the Volunteer Decoration in July 1917.

During the battle of Beersheba, on 31 October 1917, the light horse regiments were troubled all day by aircraft. Maygar had just returned to his unit after reporting to General Harry Chauvel's headquarters when the aircraft swooped using bombs and machine-guns. Maygar was hit and his horse bolted with him into the night. He was found during the night but had lost much blood and was taken to hospital at Karm. He died next day and was buried at Beersheba war cemetery (now in Israel).

In 1936 an Avenue of Honour consisting of 133 trees was dedicated at Euroa. Each tree bore a plaque in memory of a local man who had lost his life and included were three oaks dedicated to Maygar, F.H. Tubb [q.v.] and A.S. Burton [q.v.]. His name and those of the other two Victoria Cross winners are also commemorated on the Euroa War Memorial. A nearby hill was officially named Maygar Hill at the time.

Maygar's medals, including the Victoria Cross, are displayed in the Australian War Memorial's Hall of Valour.

ROGERS James

RANK	Sergeant
UNIT	South African Constabulary
DATE	15 June 1901
PLACE	Thaba 'Nchu, Orange Free State

JAMES ROGERS was born on 2 June 1875, at Moama, New South Wales. He moved with his father to Heywood in Victoria when aged eleven. Here he joined the local company of the Victorian Mounted Rifles, and by the time he had enlisted in the 1st Victorian Mounted Infantry Company, in 1899, had amassed considerable military skills. He arrived in South Africa in November 1899 and his contingent was allotted to a composite Australian regiment which saw service in the Cape Colony and Orange River areas. When the contingent returned to Australia Rogers remained behind and joined the South African Constabulary, and by June 1901 had attained the rank of sergeant.

On 15 June 1901 he was one of a party of seven men under Lieutenant F. Dickinson who were part of the rearguard to Captain Sitwell's column, a 'skirmishing party' which disposed of small groups of enemy known to have infiltrated back into territory from which they had earlier been driven. Near Thaba 'Nchu the rearguard was attacked by about fifty Boers. Lieutenant Dickinson's horse was shot and he was compelled to follow his men on foot. Rogers reined his horse in, and returned to fetch the officer, firing from his saddle as he rode. He took Dickinson up behind him and carried him 800 metres to safety. Although continually under heavy rifle fire Rogers returned on two occasions to within 350 metres of the enemy to pick up unhorsed men. The Boers called on Rogers to surrender but his answer was to continue firing. He caught two riderless horses and helped another two men to mount and ride to safety.

Dickinson reported on Rogers's gallantry and a recommendation for the Victoria Cross was forwarded. A request submitted on 10 September was returned on 7 January 1902 requesting details of previous acts of gallantry. The report was resubmitted on 24 February and Rogers's award was gazetted on 18 April 1902.

In January 1902 Rogers arrived back in Australia and was commissioned on 9 March as lieutenant in the 6th Battalion, Australian Commonwealth Horse. He was appointed to command No. 3 Troop, D Squadron from H (Hamilton District) Company, Victorian Mounted Rifles. The contingent embarked on 19 May 1902 but fighting ceased soon after their arrival in South Africa. On 7 August its members returned to Melbourne. On 18 September, Rogers was presented with the Victoria Cross by the acting governor-general, Lord Tennyson, at Government House, Melbourne.

When the 1914–18 war broke out Rogers was appointed to a commission in the 3rd Light Horse Brigade Train, AASC, with effect from 6 December 1914. He went with the brigade to Gallipoli and was wounded on 4 August 1915. After his discharge from hospital in Egypt, Rogers next served in the Anzac Provost Corps but was invalided to Australia in June 1916. His AIF appointment ended on 31 December 1916 but he remained as an honorary captain performing home service duties until the end of the war. He then held several minor appoint-

ments until transferred to the reserve of officers on 1 June 1922.

From then until his retirement Rogers ran a grazing property in the Mallee district of Victoria. He lived at Kew, Victoria, for many years before settling at Roseville, Sydney. In 1956 he and his wife attended the Victoria Cross centenary celebrations in London with the Australian contingent.

Rogers died at the Concord Repatriation Hospital in Sydney on 28 October 1961. He was survived by his wife Ethel Maud, whom he had married on 25 April 1907, and two sons. After a full military funeral on the 31st Rogers was cremated and his ashes placed in an urn in a columbarium at Springvale cemetery, Victoria. His name is also commemorated on a plaque in the Victoria Garden of Remembrance, also at Springvale.

A memorial cairn with a plaque commemorating the deeds of Rogers, erected by the citizens of Heywood and district, was unveiled on Anzac Day 1963.

WYLLY Guy George Egerton

RANK   Lieutenant

UNIT   1st Tasmanian Imperial Bushmen

DATE   1 September 1900

PLACE   Warm Bad, Transvaal

G.G.E. WYLLY was born at Hobart, Tasmania, on 17 February 1880, the son of Major Edward Arthur Egerton and Henrietta Mary Wylly. In infancy he returned to India with his parents but in 1885 the family settled at Sandy Bay, Hobart, where Wylly attended The Hutchins School. He completed his education at St Peter's College, Adelaide, then returned to Hobart. On 26 April 1900 Wylly embarked for South Africa as a lieutenant of the 1st Tasmanian Imperial Bushmen.

Wylly was one of two officers present at the same action described in Bisdee's biography. Wylly, himself wounded, saw that one of his own men, Corporal Brown, was badly wounded in the leg and was dismounted. Wylly, despite his own wound, went to the assistance of Brown. He gave his horse to Brown and, at the risk of being cut off, opened fire from behind some rocks to cover the retreat of the others. He was wounded again before transferring from the Bushmen to the South Lancashire Regiment, in which he was gazetted as second lieutenant on 5 December 1900, joining the 2nd Battalion at Jubbulpore, India. Wylly was decorated by King Edward VII at a ceremony at St James's Palace on 25 July 1902. On 1 October 1902 he transferred as a lieutenant to the Indian army and his first unit was the 46th Punjabis. On 11 February 1904, Wylly transferred to the Queen's Own Corps of Guides, and from early 1906 until September 1909 was aide-de-camp to Lord Kitchener, Commander-in-Chief, India; he was promoted to captain on 26 April 1909.

Wylly saw considerable service in the 1914–18 war as a staff officer. He was staff captain from November 1914 to September 1915 and brigade major until June 1916 with the Mhow Cavalry Brigade of the 1st Indian Cavalry Division stationed in France. He was then General Staff Officer II with the 3rd Australian Division from 10 July 1916 and with the 1st Anzac Corps from 24 February 1917. In August 1915 he was seriously wounded in the face at Authuille.

For his services in France Wylly was awarded the Distinguished Service Order in January 1918 and was twice mentioned in dispatches.

After the war Wylly returned to India and took part in several operations on the north-west frontier between 1919 and 1933. He was created Companion of the Order of the Bath that same year. His last appointment, before his retirement from the active list in November 1933 as an honorary colonel, was assistant adjutant and quartermaster general, Peshawar District, from 1929. After his retirement he lived in Britain where he died at Camberley, Surrey, on 9 January 1962. His Victoria Cross is displayed in the Tasmanian Museum and Art Gallery, Hobart.

The 1914–18 war

AXFORD Thomas Leslie

RANK Lance Corporal
UNIT 16th Battalion, 4th Brigade, 4th Division
DATE 4 July 1918
PLACE Vaire and Hamel Woods, France

'JACK' AXFORD was born on 18 June 1894, at Carrieton, South Australia, to Walter Richard and Margaret Anne Axford. He moved to Coolgardie, Western Australia, with his family when he was two and was educated there at the state school. In 1910 he went to Kalgoorlie and worked in the Boulder Brewery until he enlisted in the AIF on 9 July 1915; he had had three years' prior service with the militia in the 84th Infantry Regiment.

Axford was allotted to the 11th reinforcements of the 16th Battalion, embarked on 1 November and was taken on strength at Tel el Kebir on 7 March 1916. He was wounded twice, in August 1916 and August 1917, the latter wound keeping him out of action until January 1918. He then attended corps and gas training schools and was appointed lance corporal in February and promoted to corporal in July.

His award of the Military Medal appeared in the *London Gazette* of 13 September 1918, but no details are provided.

Axford won the Victoria Cross on 4 July during the battle of Hamel. It was a textbook victory which enhanced the reputation of General John Monash and was the model for the decisive battle of Amiens five weeks later. Axford's battalion was in the centre of the 4th Brigade's assault and its task was to clear Vaire and Hamel Woods. As the Australians advanced up a slope they encountered heavy fire from the German front line. The adjoining platoon to Axford's was delayed by the uncut wire, suffering many casualties. Axford rushed in from the flank to assist. He jumped into the enemy trench and bombed and bayoneted the machine-gun crews, killing ten enemy and taking six prisoners. He threw the machine-guns over the parapet and called the delayed platoon forward before he returned to his own platoon with which he fought for the remainder of the operation. He had previously helped lay out the assault line tapes which were within 100 metres of the enemy.

Axford returned to Australia in October 1918 and was discharged from the AIF on 6 February 1919. He enlisted in the AMF on 25 June 1941; after service with the Western Australian Echelon and Records

Office he was discharged on 14 April 1947 with the rank of sergeant.

On 27 November 1926 he married Lily Maud Foster at St Mary's Catholic Cathedral, Sydney, and they settled at Mount Hawthorn, a suburb of Perth, where Axford worked with the H.V. McKay Sunshine Harvester Company. The Axfords had a family of two sons and three daughters. In 1956 he and his wife attended the Victoria Cross centenary celebrations in London. Axford died on 11 October 1983 on a flight between Dubai and Hong Kong. He was returning home from the Victoria Cross–George Cross biennial reunion in London. His wife had predeceased him.

BEATHAM Robert Matthew

RANK	Private
UNIT	8th Battalion, 2nd Brigade, 1st Division
DATE	9 August 1918
PLACE	Rosières, east of Villers-Bretonneux, France

ROBERT BEATHAM was born at Glassonby, Cumberland, UK, on 16 June 1894, son of John and Elizabeth Beatham. While still in his teens he migrated alone to Australia and was working at Geelong, Victoria, as a labourer when he enlisted in the AIF on 8 January 1915.

He embarked for Egypt in April but returned to Australia for medical reasons in July. He re-embarked in September with the 8th reinforcements for the 8th Battalion, arrived in Suez early in October, and was taken on strength on 7 December. In early 1916 Beatham sailed with his battalion to France where he was twice wounded in action — at Pozières in August 1916 and Passchendaele in October 1917.

The 1st Division fought in Flanders from April to August 1918. It rejoined the Australian Corps on the Somme on the second day of the battle of Amiens. Because of a long approach march the 1st Division could not reach its starting line on time so the 15th Brigade took over and achieved the first Australian objective that day. About 1.40 p.m. the 2nd Brigade passed through the 15th Brigade and continued the attack towards Lihons. When the 8th Battalion was held up Beatham, assisted by Lance Corporal Nottingham, rushed forward and bombed and fought the crews of four guns, killing ten and capturing ten others, thus allowing the advance to continue and saving many casualties. On 11 August, when the battalion neared its objective on the southern slope of Lihons, it was again halted by German reinforcements. Beatham, though wounded, rushed another machine-gun and bombed and silenced it. In doing so he was riddled with bullets and killed. He was buried at Heath cemetery, Harbonnières. The Victoria Cross was awarded posthumously and was received by his mother from King George V at Buckingham Palace on 8 March 1919. His Victoria Cross was sold in a London auction in 1967.

BIRKS Frederick

RANK	Second Lieutenant
UNIT	6th Battalion, 2nd Brigade, 1st Division
DATE	20 September 1917
PLACE	Glencorse Wood, east of Ypres, Belgium

FREDERICK BIRKS was born on 16 August 1894 at Buckley, Flintshire, UK, third of seven children of Samuel and Mary Birks. His father died in a coalmining accident in 1902 when Frederick was eight. Educated at the local St Matthew's Anglican parish school, he later worked for John Summers & Sons as a labourer and steel-rollerman in the nearby town of Shotton. He and his friend Emrys Jones migrated to Australia in 1913. Birks worked as a labourer in Tasmania, South Australia and Victoria, but he was working as a waiter in Melbourne when he enlisted in the AIF on 18 August 1914. He was posted to the 2nd Field Ambulance, AAMC, and sailed for Egypt in

October. His unit went into action at Gallipoli on 25 April 1915 where it provided medical support for the 2nd Infantry Brigade. On 26 June Birks, a stretcher bearer, was wounded by shrapnel but he resumed duty next day and remained at Anzac until 9 September. He went to France with the 2nd Field Ambulance in March 1916, was promoted to lance corporal on 21 April and served throughout the first battle of the Somme as a stretcher bearer. At Pozières on 26 July he was awarded an immediate Military Medal by General William Birdwood for continually leading his squad of stretcher bearers through the wood and village of Pozières from the front line while the area was being heavily shelled.

Promoted to corporal on 10 August 1916, Birks was selected for officer training in February 1917 and was commissioned second lieutenant on 26 April, joining the 6thBattalion on 12 May.

The third battle of Ypres opened on 31 July. Rain on the first day turned the battlefield into a quagmire and the August attacks failed. When the ground dried the new tactic of wearing the enemy down in a series of battles or steps was adopted. The first step, the battle of Menin Road, saw the 1st and 2nd Australian Divisions going in side by side on 20 September. The 6th Battalion was to take the 2nd Brigade's first objective. It was Birks's first major engagement as an infantry officer. His battalion was advancing on Glencorse Wood when Birks and a corporal rushed a pillbox which was delaying the advance. The corporal was wounded. Birks went on alone, killed the enemy occupying the position and captured a machine-gun. Soon after he organized a small party to take out another strong point, occupied by about twenty-five of the enemy, and succeeded in inflicting nine casualties and capturing sixteen men. In the consolidation which followed, Birks reorganized groups from other units which were in disarray. The following day Birks (and four others) were killed during an artillery bombardment while he was attempting to rescue some of his men who had been buried by a shell explosion. He was buried in China Wall (Zillebeke) cemetery, Belgium.

His older brother, Samuel Birks, MSM, served in the Royal Artillery as a sergeant in France and Italy. He was recalled from Italy to receive his brother's posthumously awarded Victoria Cross from King George V on 19 December 1917.

In 1921 a cenotaph was erected in Birks's honour outside St Matthew's school, Buckley. The school has since been demolished and the cenotaph now stands in front of St Matthew's Church. His portrait by F. Hornsby and his Victoria Cross are in the collection of the Australian War Memorial, Canberra. The Victoria Cross, presented in 1972, is on display in the Hall of Valour.

BLACKBURN Arthur Seaforth

RANK	Lieutenant
UNIT	10th Battalion, 3rd Brigade, 1st Division
DATE	23 July 1916
PLACE	Pozières, France

ARTHUR BLACKBURN was born on 25 November 1892 at Woodville, South Australia, youngest child of Canon Thomas and Margaret Harriet Blackburn. He was educated at Pulteney Grammar School, the Collegiate School of St Peter and Adelaide University. He graduated Bachelor of Laws in 1913 and was called to the bar in December of that year.

On 19 August 1914 he left the Adelaide legal firm he was working in and enlisted in the AIF, embarking for Egypt in late October aboard HMAT A11 (*Ascanius*). He landed at Gallipoli on 25 April 1915 and on this first day he and Private Phil Robin distinguished themselves by penetrating 1800 metres inland from Anzac Cove, reaching a point further than any other Australian soldier was to achieve in the campaign. A few days later he was appointed lance corporal and in August was commissioned second lieutenant; on 26 February 1916 he was promoted to lieutenant and later he embarked for France.

The 10th Battalion was in reserve when the 1st Division attacked Pozières at 12.30 a.m. on 23 July 1916. The 9th Battalion had met strong opposition and asked for assistance. A company of the 10th were detached for this purpose. At 5.30 a.m. the 10th was asked for further assistance as the advance was being held up by furious machine-gun fire. Blackburn and fifty men of D Company were detailed to report to the 9th and ordered to move on the trench where, several hours earlier, John Leak had won the Victoria Cross. D Company were to drive the enemy out. This they did after Blackburn personally led four successive bombing parties, many members of which were killed; the enemy strong point was destroyed and nearly 350 metres of trench were captured. Blackburn was supported by his platoon sergeant, R.M. Inwood (whose brother Corporal Reg Inwood would win the Victoria Cross in 1917), until Inwood was killed. For this exploit Blackburn was awarded the Victoria Cross for 'most conspicuous bravery'. In September he was evacuated sick and on 4 October 1916 was invested by King George V at Buckingham Palace.

Invalided to Adelaide, on 22 March 1917 Blackburn married Rose Ada Kelly, and on 10 April was discharged from the AIF on medical grounds. He returned to legal practice and took an active part in the pro-conscription campaigns. From 1918 to 1921 he was National member for Sturt in the House of Assembly where his speeches usually related to serving and returned soldiers. He was a founding member of the Returned Sailors', Soldiers' and Airmen's Imperial League in South Australia and president in 1920–21. In 1925 he and a former comrade from the 10th Battalion, W.F.J. McCann, MC, became partners in a legal practice. On 9 September 1933 Blackburn was appointed city coroner, a position he held for fourteen years.

Blackburn's militia service began on 31 October 1925 when he went into the 43rd Battalion as a lieutenant. He was promoted to captain in 1927 and on 1 July 1928 was transferred to a light horse regiment. He was promoted to major on 15 January 1937 and on 1 July 1939 was appointed to command the 18th Light Horse (Machine Gun) Regiment. When the second world war began he formed the 2/3rd Machine Gun Battalion, AIF, which he led during the Syrian campaign in 1941. Blackburn, as the senior British officer present, accepted the surrender of Damascus on 21 June. He later presided over a committee of the Syrian Commission of Control dealing with the problems of prisoners. In February 1942 Blackburn and his battalion were among 7th Division troops hastily landed in Java. He was promoted to temporary brigadier and appointed to command Blackforce, an *ad hoc* brigade-size group, with orders to assist the Dutch against the rapid Japanese advance. After three weeks' vigorous but fruitless resistance, the Allied forces surrendered. Blackburn was imprisoned by the Japanese in Singapore, Moji in southern Japan, Pusan in Korea, and finally Mukden (Shenyang), Manchuria, where he was liberated in September 1945. In 1946 he was appointed CBE (Military) for distinguished service in Java.

From 1947 to 1955 Blackburn served as a commissioner in the Commonwealth Court of Conciliation and Arbitration. In 1955 he became a member of the Australian National Airlines Commission and a company director. He had again been state president of the Returned Services League from 1946 until 1949, and was chairman of the Services Canteen Trust Fund from 1947 to his death; for these and other community services he was made CMG in 1955. The following year he attended the gathering of Victoria Cross winners in London. He died suddenly at Crafers of a burst aneurism on 24 November 1960, and was survived by his wife, two sons and two daughters. He was buried with full military honours in West Terrace cemetery, Adelaide.

BORELLA Albert Chalmers

RANK   Lieutenant
UNIT   26th Battalion, 7th Brigade, 2nd Division
DATE   17–18 July 1918
PLACE   Villers-Bretonneux, France

ALBERT BORELLA was born on 7 August 1881 at Borung, Victoria, son of Louis and Annie Borella. His mother died when he was four and his father remarried. He was educated at Borung and Wychitella state schools. He later farmed in the Borung and Echuca districts, and also served for eighteen months with a volunteer infantry regiment, the Victorian Rangers.

From April 1910 until January 1913 Borella was employed by the Metropolitan Fire Brigade Board, Melbourne. He then took up a pastoral lease, drawn by ballot, on the Daly River, Northern Territory, where, with the help of Aboriginals, he built a house and partly fenced his holding before costs forced him to abandon it early in 1915. On 15 March he enlisted in the AIF and was posted to B Company, 26th Battalion, on 24 May. After training in Egypt his unit landed at Gallipoli on 12 September. Borella, however, did not serve there as he had been admitted to hospital on the 8th and did not rejoin his unit until 5 February 1916.

His unit sailed for France in March and Borella, now lance sergeant, was wounded in the battle of Pozières Heights on 29 July, and was evacuated. He was promoted to sergeant in January 1917, and although recommended for a higher award was mentioned in dispatches in February for 'devotion to duty and general good work in the trenches', and the following month was awarded the Military Medal for conspicuous bravery in action during the attack on Malt trench, north of Warlencourt. He was commissioned second lieutenant on 7 April and in August was sent to Britain for officer training and promoted to lieutenant.

The 2nd Division moved from Flanders and took up positions near Dernancourt in early April 1918. It was mainly engaged with patrolling and raids that gained ground piecemeal from the Germans. Borella was involved in this fighting which continued into July when the division moved south of the Somme into positions east of Villers-Bretonneux. On 17 July, in a further advance, Borella was initially recommended for the Distinguished Service Order, but the award was upgraded to a Victoria

Cross by higher authority. While leading his platoon in an assault on an enemy support trench, he noticed a machine-gun firing through the Australian barrage and ran out ahead of his men into the barrage, shot the gunners with his revolver and captured the gun. He then led a small party against strongly held Jaffa trench, 200 metres beyond his actual objective. A sharp fight ensued and the surprised defenders were showered with bombs and Lewis gun fire with the result that thirty Germans emerged from two dug-outs and were taken prisoner. Borella and his twenty or so men had to withdraw after persistent counter-attacks which resulted in heavy losses for the enemy. Several weeks later Borella was evacuated sick and was invalided to Australia on 6 November 1918. His AIF appointment ended on 23 February 1919.

From 1920 to 1939 Borella farmed on a soldier settlement block near Hamilton, Victoria, and on 16 August 1928 married Elsie Jane Love at Wesley Church, Hamilton. He was National Party candidate for Dundas in the 1924 Legislative Assembly election and was only narrowly defeated. In September 1939 he changed his name by deed poll, and he and his family used the surname Chalmers-Borella.

On 15 October 1939 Borella was appointed, from the reserve of officers, lieutenant in the 12th Australian Garrison Battalion with which he served until 1941 when he was attached to the Prisoner of War Group, Rushworth. Promoted to temporary captain on 2 January 1942, he was later promoted to captain on 1 September 1942. He next served with the 51st Garrison Company at Myrtleford from March 1943 until discharged in 1945. Borella then moved to Albury, New South Wales, joined the Commonwealth Department of Supply and Shipping, and was an inspector of dangerous cargoes until he retired in 1956. Survived by his wife and two of his four sons, he died at his home in North Albury on 7 February 1968 and was buried with full military honours in the Presbyterian cemetery.

When he gained his Victoria Cross, this quietly spoken, unostentatious man was approaching his thirty-seventh birthday, and was thus the oldest member of the first AIF to be so decorated. A painting by his niece was presented to the city of Albury in 1966. In 1977 a street in Albury was renamed Borella Road in his honour and a plaque unveiled on a memorial nearby, where the road begins.

BROWN Walter Ernest

RANK	Corporal
UNIT	20th Battalion, 5th Brigade, 2nd Division
DATE	6 July 1918
PLACE	Villers-Bretonneux, France

'WALLY' BROWN was born on 3 July 1885 at New Norfolk, Tasmania, son of Sidney Francis and Agnes Mary Brown. He was brought up at New Norfolk and on leaving school worked as a grocer, first in Hobart until 1911, and in Petersham, New South Wales, until the first world war.

Brown enlisted in the AIF on 26 July 1915, embarked for Egypt in October and joined the 1st Light Horse Regiment on 14 January 1916. In July, hoping to be transferred to the infantry in France, he invented a story of having lost his false teeth so that he would be sent to Cairo. Here he obtained a transfer to the 20th Battalion reinforcements. On 30 Sep-tember he sailed for France, served for a month with the 55th Battalion, for six months with the 1st and 2nd Australian Field Butcheries, and joined the 20th Battalion at St Omer on 8 August 1917. In September and October he fought at Passchendaele and was awarded the Distinguished Conduct Medal for attending wounded under heavy fire and, after his sergeant had been disabled, tak-ing charge of the section and display-ing a fine example of courage and leadership. During the battle his close friend went missing. Brown refused leave so that he might search the battlefield for his friend's body. He found the body in a temporary grave and erected a cross over it before he returned to duty. Pro-moted to lance corporal on 19 October, he was slightly wounded in November.

In April 1918 the 2nd Division moved from Flanders to Dernan-court where it engaged the Germans with peaceful penetration tactics that gained ground a little at a time. In July the 2nd Division moved south of the Somme and on the 6th his unit relieved one of the battalions that had taken part in the textbook vic-tory at Hamel. Brown, who had been promoted to corporal on 7 April, was with an advance party which took over some newly captured trenches near Accroche Wood and, on being told that a sniper's post was causing trouble, he located the enemy strong point, picked up two Mills bombs and ran towards it under fire. His first bomb fell short, but on reaching the post he knocked one German down with his fist and threatened the others with the remaining Mills bomb. The whole party, consisting of one officer and twelve men of the 137th Infantry Regiment, surrendered and Brown shepherded them back to the Australian lines.

He was twice wounded on 11 August and rejoined his unit on 26 August. Brown left shortly after to go on leave before returning to Australia. He was promoted to sergeant on 13 September. Brown was discharged from the AIF in February 1920 and for the next ten years worked in Sydney as a brass-finisher and, for the ten years after that, at Leeton as a water bailiff with the New South Wales Water Conservation and Irrigation Commission.

Brown married Maude Dillon at Bexley on 4 June 1932. On 21 June 1940, by giving his age as thirty-nine instead of fifty-four, Brown enlisted in the second AIF. His real age and record were soon discovered, and he was promoted to lance sergeant and posted to the 2/15th Field Regiment, but reverted to gunner at his own request. The regiment, part of the ill-fated 8th Division, reached Malaya in August 1941. Brown was last seen a few hours before the surrender to the Japanese at Singapore, when he picked up some grenades and walked towards the enemy lines with the parting comment 'No surrender for me'. It is likely that he was killed shortly afterwards on the evening of 15 February 1942. His body was never recovered. His name is commemorated on the Singapore Memorial. The Leeton Soldiers' Club have erected a special plaque to his memory. He was survived by his wife, a son and a daughter.

His medals and a machine-gun he captured are displayed in the Hall of Valour at the Australian War Memorial as is his portrait by John Longstaff.

BUCKLEY Alexander Henry

RANK   Temporary Corporal
UNIT   54th Battalion, 14th Brigade, 5th Division
DATE   1 September 1918
PLACE   Péronne, France

ALEX BUCKLEY was born on 22 July 1891 at Warren, New South Wales, fourth child of James and Julia Buckley. He was educated at home by his parents and later farmed with his father on Homebush, a property near Gulargambone, in the Coonamble district of New South Wales.

On 3 February 1916, at Dubbo, he

enlisted in the AIF and embarked for Britain in June with the 3rd reinforcements for the 54th Battalion. He joined the battalion at Flers, France, on 17 November, served on the Somme in the winter of 1916–17 and in 1917 fought at Bullecourt, Polygon Wood and Broodseinde. He was made temporary corporal in November. In April 1918 his unit moved into the Villers-Bretonneux sector and in August took part in the Allied counter-offensive.

On 1 September Buckley's battalion was involved in operations aimed at clearing the area between Mont St Quentin and Péronne. The 54th was to take the ground between Péronne and the River Somme, then move in on Péronne if not too strongly opposed. The advance commenced in drizzling rain and was opposed by heavy fire. The first line of enemy trenches was taken but the advance was held up by a nest of machine-gunners. Buckley with another man rushed the post, shooting four men and taking twenty-two prisoners. From another direction this same trench was being attacked by Corporal A.C.Hall [q.v.]. The Germans retreated to Péronne, entering the city by the main bridge which they then destroyed. The only remaining bridge on the battalion's front was a footbridge defended by machine-guns. With three other members of his company, Buckley tried to force his way across under heavy fire. He was killed in the attempt. Of the three other members, two were killed but Lieutenant J. Adams, MC and bar, survived. The battalion moved into Péronne which surren-

dered twenty minutes later, although mopping up continued into the next day.

Buckley was awarded his Victoria Cross for his 'initiative, resource and courage'. He was buried in the Péronne communal cemetery extension, Ste Radegonde.

BUCKLEY Maurice Vincent (alias **SEXTON**, Gerald)

RANK   Sergeant
UNIT   13th Battalion, 4th Brigade, 4th Division
DATE   18 September 1918
PLACE   Near Le Verguier, north-west of St Quentin, France

MAURICE BUCKLEY was born on 13 April 1891 at Hawthorn, Victoria, son of Timothy and Honora Mary Agnes Buckley. Educated at the

Christian Brothers' school, Abbotsford, he became a coach-trimmer and was working at Warrnambool when he enlisted in the AIF on 18 December 1914. The following June he embarked for Egypt with reinforcements for the 13th Light Horse Regiment but subsequently returned to Australia and was admitted to Langwarrin Camp on 25 September 1915. He deserted from Langwarrin on 21 January 1916, was declared a deserter and struck off strength on 20 March.

He re-enlisted under the alias of Gerald Sexton on 6 May 1916; Gerald was the name of his brother who had been accidently killed six months before, shortly after joining the AIF, and Sexton was his mother's maiden name. He embarked for France in October with the 13th Battalion reinforcements and joined his unit on the Somme in January 1917. That year he fought at Bullecourt, Polygon Wood, Ypres and Passchendaele and, early in 1918, at Hébuterne and Villers-Bretonneux. He was promoted to lance corporal in January and by June was a lance sergeant in charge of a Lewis gun section. On 6 July Buckley, now a temporary sergeant, was wounded at Hamel but resumed duty for the Allied offensive on 8 August in which he won the Distinguished Conduct Medal. When his company was delayed by sudden machine-gun fire during the advance from Hamel towards Morcourt, Buckley quickly silenced each enemy post by using his Lewis gun with promptness and skill. On one occasion, when his unit was advancing through tall crops, a

hidden gun caused several casualties. Buckley stood up in full view of the enemy, calmly noted the position of the gun from the flashes and, firing from the hip, put it out of action. He was confirmed as sergeant on 28 August.

On 18 September the 13th Battalion took part in the attack on Le Verguier. The battalion set off behind a creeping barrage and cleared several enemy outposts, two of which fell to Buckley's Lewis gun. When a field gun held up one company he rushed towards it, shot the crew and raced under machine-gun fire across open ground to put a trench mortar out of action. He then fired into an enemy dug-out and captured thirty Germans. By the end of the day he had rushed at least six machine-gun positions, captured a field gun and taken nearly 100 prisoners. The award of the Victoria Cross for these actions was gazetted under the name Sexton, but soon after a notice appeared in the *London Gazette* that his correct name was Maurice Vincent Buckley. He was invested by King George V at Buckingham Palace on 29 May 1919.

Buckley returned to Australia on 8 September 1919 and was discharged as medically unfit in December. The following year he began work as a road contractor in Gippsland. In February 1920, he had been a member of a delegation that had approached the Melbourne City Council requesting permission to hold the traditional St Patrick's day march the following month. Several anti-Catholic and anti-Irish groups wanted to stop the march. Speaking in support of the march, Buckley said that his Victoria Cross was his 'most treasured possession; yet I pledge it to you [Melbourne City Council] that we will loyally abide by your ruling'. Permission was granted and one of the most memorable marches took place when Buckley and thirteen other Victoria Cross winners, leading 10 000 Catholic ex-servicemen and women, marched in honour of the Catholic Archbishop of Melbourne, Daniel Mannix.

On 15 January 1921 Buckley was injured when he tried to jump his horse over the railway gates at Boolarra, Victoria. He was operated on in Fitzroy, appeared to recover, but relapsed and died on 27 January. After a requiem mass in St Patrick's Cathedral, Buckley was buried in Brighton cemetery with full military honours, ten Victoria Cross winners acting as pallbearers. Buckley was unmarried. The medals of this modest, unassuming and very brave man are displayed in the Australian War Memorial Hall of Valour.

BUGDEN Patrick Joseph

RANK	Private
UNIT	31st Battalion, 8th Brigade, 5th Division
DATE	26–28 September 1917
PLACE	Polygon Wood, near Ypres, Belgium

PAT BUGDEN was born on 17 March 1897 at South Gundurimba, New South Wales, eldest child of Thomas and Annie Bugden. His father died when Bugden was six, leaving four children, and his mother remarried. He was educated at Gundurimba public school and the convent school at Tatham. He later worked for his stepfather as a barman at the Federal Hotel, Alstonville. He enlisted at Lismore on 25 May 1916, stating his occupation as hotelkeeper; his previous military training had consisted of twelve months' service under the compulsory system, 'boy conscription', introduced in 1911.

Bugden trained at Enoggera, Queensland, before embarking for the western front with the 31st Battalion reinforcements in September. He joined the unit at Bapaume on 19 March 1917 and was continually in action until the end of May. The division was rested until September when it relieved the 1st Division after their successful Menin Road battle.

The next step was taken by the 4th and 5th Divisions on 26 September, the battle of Polygon Wood. The 8th Brigade, which included the 31st Battalion, was to be in reserve for this battle. The day before the battle the Germans launched an attack on the 33rd British Division immediately to the south of the 5th Division. The 5th Division's 15th Brigade was badly shelled and found its flank exposed as the British withdrew. The decision was made to launch the attack on schedule the next day and the 31st Battalion was brought up to take the 15th Brigade's first objective.

On two occasions, when the advance was held up by pillboxes, Bugden led small parties to attack these strong points which he successfully silenced with bombs and by capturing their garrisons at bayonet point. In the next two days he performed several additional acts of gallantry. His most audacious act was his single-handed rescue of a corporal who was being escorted into the German lines by three enemy soldiers. On at least five other occasions he dashed out into intense shell and machine-gun fire to bring in wounded. He was killed on 28 September and for his bravery during these three days Bugden was

awarded a posthumous Victoria Cross.

Bugden was buried in Hooge Crater cemetery, Zillebeke, Belgium. He was unmarried. On 14 June 1980, his sister, Mrs R.C. Elliott, presented his Victoria Cross to the Queensland Museum for display in their new building.

BURTON Alexander Stewart

RANK   Corporal
UNIT   7th Battalion, 2nd Brigade, 1st Division
DATE   9 August 1915
PLACE   Lone Pine trenches, Gallipoli Peninsula, Turkey

ALEXANDER BURTON was born at Kyneton, Victoria, on 20 January 1893 to Alfred Edward and Isabella Burton. After attending the state

43

school he worked as an ironmonger at Euroa. Burton was a chorister in the Euroa Presbyterian Church, a member of the town band and a keen sportsman. In 1911 he began his period of compulsory military service.

Burton enlisted on 18 August 1914 and joined the 7th Battalion, commanded by Colonel H.E. Elliott, and embarked at Melbourne on 19 October for Egypt. Training at Mena, Egypt, was interrupted briefly when the 7th and 8th Battalions moved to Ismailia when the Turks threatened the Suez Canal.

At the Anzac landing on 25 April, Burton, ill with a throat infection, watched the landing from a hospital ship. A week later he was ashore. He was slightly wounded in action and in July was promoted to lance corporal and, not long after, to corporal. It was during the Turkish counter-attack on the Lone Pine trenches on 9 August that he performed the actions for which he was posthumously awarded the Victoria Cross. The Turks advanced up a sap and blew in a sandbag barricade which Burton, Tubb [q.v.] and Dunstan [q.v.] quickly re-erected after they had repulsed the attackers. The enemy attacked twice more and destroyed the barricade. This was rebuilt when the enemy were driven off. Burton was killed by one of several bombs which exploded as he was attempting to rebuild the parapet. On 28 January 1916 he was mentioned in dispatches.

In November 1936 Burton was honoured in the Avenue of Honour in Euroa along with L.C. Maygar

and F.H. Tubb. Later a bridge over nearby Seven Creeks was officially renamed Burton Bridge. His name is also commemorated on the Lone Pine Memorial on Gallipoli. Seven Victoria Crosses were awarded during the fighting at Lone Pine and Burton's is one of five of these which are displayed together in the Australian War Memorial's Hall of Valour. He was unmarried.

CARROLL John

RANK	Private
UNIT	33rd Battalion, 9th Brigade, 3rd Division
DATE	7–10 June 1917
PLACE	St Yves, Belgium (battle of Messines Ridge)

JOHN CARROLL was born on 16 August 1891 in Brisbane, Queensland, son of John and Catherine Carroll. When he was two years old the family moved to Donnybrook, Western Australia, and then to Yarloop. About 1905 they settled at Kurrawang where John and his father joined the Goldfields Firewood Supply Co. as labourers. Tall and well built, John was a good athlete and a prominent member of the local football club. He was working as a railway guard on the Kurrawang line when he enlisted in the AIF on 27 April 1916.

Carroll embarked for Britain in August with reinforcements for the 44th Battalion, then on 14 November was transferred to the 33rd Battalion. He went into the line at Armentières, France, and served there until April 1917 when his unit moved into position for the Messines offensive. On 7 June, in the battle of Messines Ridge, immediately the barrage lifted, Carroll rushed an enemy trench and bayoneted four men, then rescued a comrade who was in difficulties. Later in the advance he attacked a machine-gun crew of four, killing three of the crew and capturing the gun, and, in spite of heavy shelling and machine-gun fire, dug out two members of his battalion who had been buried by a shell explosion. During the battle his battalion was in action for four days and Carroll exhibited courage and fearlessness throughout. For this he was awarded the Victoria Cross. He was wounded in July and in September was promoted to lance corporal; on 12 October, in the second battle of Passchendaele, he was severely wounded. He was decorated by King George V at Buckingham Palace on 23 March 1918, and did not rejoin his unit until June. The following month he was transferred to AIF Headquarters, London, and in August returned to Australia.

After demobilization Carroll resumed work as a guard on the Kurrawang line. He married Mary Brown at the Catholic Cathedral, Perth, on 23 April 1923; they had no children. In the mid-1920s he moved to the Yarloop district and in 1927, when he was working as a railway truck examiner at Hoffman Mill, he had one foot badly crushed. The foot was amputated, but he continued working for many years as a labourer and railway employee. In 1956 he went to the Victoria Cross centenary celebrations in London, then retired to the Perth suburb of Bedford. He died in the Repatriation General Hospital, Hollywood, Perth, on 4 October 1971 and was buried in Karrakatta cemetery with full military honours. His wife had predeceased him.

CARTWRIGHT George

RANK	Private
UNIT	33rd Battalion, 9th Brigade, 3rd Division
DATE	31 August 1918
PLACE	Rood Wood, south-west of Bouchavesnes, near Péronne, France

GEORGE CARTWRIGHT was born at South Kensington, London, UK, on 9 December 1894, son of N.E. Cartwright. He migrated by himself to Australia and worked as a labourer in the Elsmore district of New South Wales. On 9 December 1915 he enlisted in the AIF at Inverell, was allotted to the 33rd Battalion, and embarked on 4 May 1916 for Britain. The 33rd left for France in November and in the following June Cartwright was wounded and away from his unit for a month. He was gassed in April 1918, rejoined his battalion late in June, and went through the August offensive unscathed until 30 September when he was again wounded.

Cartwright received his Victoria Cross for conspicuous bravery on the last day of August during the attack on Rood Wood, south-west of Bouchavesnes, near Péronne. When two companies were held up by withering machine-gun fire, Cartwright rushed forward again and threw a bomb at the post, then captured the gun and nine prisoners. Cartwright's gallantry had a most inspiring effect upon the rest of the battalion who stood up and cheered and renewed the attack with vigour.

The wounds Cartwright received necessitated hospital treatment in Britain; he was discharged for duty in January 1919. He received his Victoria Cross from King George V at Buckingham Palace on 8 March and later that month was repatriated to Australia and discharged in Sydney on 1 July.

After his return to civilian life Cartwright maintained his interest in military activities by joining the 3rd Battalion (Werriwa Regiment) of the Citizen Military Forces, in which he rose to the rank of sergeant. After the 3rd was linked with the 4th Battalion to form the 4th/3rd Battalion, Cartwright was further promoted to warrant rank, and, on 25 February 1932, was appointed lieutenant. In October 1936 the 3rd Battalion was reactivated as a separate unit and Cartwright continued his service in the 4th (The Australian Rifles), except for a break from 1937 to 1938. In October 1939 he was promoted to temporary captain and from March 1940 to September 1943 was seconded for duty with the Reception Training Depot in Eastern Command. For part of this time he was engaged in training reinforcements for the AIF at Tamworth and also served with the 112th Convalescent Depot. From September 1943 to September 1945 Cartwright was second-in-command of the 28th Infantry Training Battalion, after which he transferred to the Australian Army Amenities Service until his demobilization in May 1946. In April 1955 he received the Efficiency Decoration for his CMF service.

Cartwright visited London for the Victoria Cross centenary celebrations in 1956. He lived in Epping, New South Wales, until his death on 2 February 1978. He was cremated in a private ceremony. His name is commemorated in the New South Wales Garden of Remembrance at Rookwood.

The machine-gun captured by Cartwright on 31 August 1918 is displayed in the Hall of Valour at the Australian War Memorial and his Victoria Cross and other medals are displayed in the Imperial War Museum, London.

CASTLETON Claud Charles

RANK   Sergeant
UNIT   5th Machine Gun Company, 5th Brigade, 2nd Division
DATE   28 July 1916
PLACE Pozières, France

CLAUD CASTLETON was born at Kirkley, Lowestoft, Suffolk, UK, on 12 April 1893, son of Thomas Charles and Edith Lucy Castleton. He was educated at Lowestoft municipal secondary school and worked as a pupil-teacher in the local council school before migrating to Australia at the age of nineteen. Arriving in Melbourne in 1912, his interest in nature and geography led him to undertake extensive travels which included Tasmania and the eastern states.

When the first world war broke out Castleton was in Port Moresby. He offered his services to the Papuan administration and worked with native troops preparing for coastal defence; he also worked at the Moresby radio station. In March 1915 he returned to Sydney and enlisted in the AIF on the 10th, stating his occupation as prospector. He was posted to the 18th Battalion and sailed for Egypt in June. The first elements of his unit reached Gallipoli on 6 August and were allotted to the 2nd Brigade until the remainder of the battalion arrived on 19 August. On 22 August the battalion attacked Hill 60 and although it suffered 50 per cent casualties it remained at Gallipoli until the evacuation.

Castleton was promoted to corporal on 7 December and to temporary sergeant in February 1916. On 8 March, soon after his arrival in France, he was transferred to the 5th Machine Gun Company and was confirmed in his rank on the 16th.

From 25 until 27 July the 2nd Division replaced the 1st Division, then facing Pozières Heights. The division tried to assault Pozières Heights at 12.15 a.m. on the morning of 28 July, but was repulsed. The troops were pinned down by machine-gun fire but in the comparative quiet in the hour before dawn most were withdrawn. Some wounded were left in no man's land. Castleton went out twice and brought in wounded men, but while bringing in a third he was hit in the back and killed instantly. He was awarded the Victoria Cross posthumously for his splendid example of courage and self-sacrifice, and was buried in the Pozières British cemetery at Ovillers-la-Boiselle, France. He was unmarried.

CHERRY Percy Herbert

RANK Captain
UNIT 26th Battalion, 7th Brigade, 2nd Division
DATE 26 March 1917
PLACE Lagnicourt, France

PERCY CHERRY was born on 4 June 1895 at Drysdale, Victoria, son of John Gawley and Elizabeth Cherry. When he was seven the family moved to Tasmania and took up an apple orchard at Cradoc. Percy attended the local state school until he was thirteen and was then privately tutored. He played the cornet in the Franklin brass band, sang in the Anglican church choir and served in the local cadet corps. He worked with his father and became an expert apple packer and at fourteen won a local case-making championship at the Launceston fruit show. In 1913 he was commissioned in the 93rd Infantry Regiment.

At Franklin on 5 March 1915 Cherry enlisted in the AIF and was posted to the 26th Battalion; although he was a qualified infantry officer he was considered too young for an AIF appointment and he sailed for Egypt in June as a quartermaster sergeant. In August he was made a company sergeant major and next month reached Gallipoli where he served at Taylor's Hollow and Russell's Top. He was wounded just before the evacuation, on 1 December, and a week later was promoted to second lieutenant.

In March 1916 Cherry attended a machine-gun course and was transferred to the 7th Machine Gun Company and sent to France. He commanded the company's 1st Battery at Armentières and Messines and on the Somme until 5 August when he was wounded in a duel with a German officer at Pozières. After sniping at each other from their shell-holes both officers fired simultaneously and both were wounded, the German mortally. Cherry went over to his opponent and was given a package of letters which he promised to post. The German's dying words were 'and so it ends'. Cherry was promoted to lieutenant on 25 August and resumed active duty in November. Next month he was made temporary captain and transferred back to the 26th Battalion as a company commander.

Cherry's rank was confirmed on 14 February 1917.

In order to shorten the line and save troops, as well as dislocate expected allied attacks, the Germans started to withdraw to the Hindenburg line in stages during February 1917. The first withdrawal left the Germans in front of Bapaume. The 6th Australian Brigade attacked Malt trench between Warlencourt and Bapaume on 25 February but was not successful. The 7th Australian Brigade attacked the same position at 3 a.m. on 2 March. As the wire in front of Cherry's company was not cut, he led them in single file through a cut in the wire of the neighbouring company's area to move into the attack. He rushed two machine-gun posts, capturing one single-handed and turning the gun on the fleeing Germans before being wounded himself. He was awarded the Military Cross for this action although he was never to know.

The Germans left strongly entrenched garrisons at almost every village in order to delay the approach to the Hindenburg line. On 26 March 1917 Cherry's battalion was ordered to storm the village of Lagnicourt. Cherry's company encountered fierce opposition and when all the other officers had been killed or wounded he led his men forward and cleared the enemy from the village. At one stage a stoutly defended crater temporarily checked the attackers. Cherry sent for mortars but before they were brought down on the crater Cherry rushed the position under Lewis gun and rifle grenade cover. After the crater was taken Cherry and his party pushed on through the village. Sensing the possibility of counter-attacks, he kept his party in position to strengthen the sector. The Germans did counter-attack and the battle raged all day long. Next day the Germans shelled the Australian positions kil-

49

ling Cherry among others. Cherry was buried in the Queant Road cemetery, Buissy. He was awarded the Victoria Cross, an honour for which his battalion commander had recommended him for 'bravery beyond description'. Cherry was unmarried.

His Victoria Cross, Military Cross and service medals are displayed in the Australian War Memorial's Hall of Valour.

COOKE Thomas

RANK   Private
UNIT   8th Battalion, 2nd
       Brigade, 1st Division
DATE   24–25 July 1916
PLACE Pozières, France

TOM COOKE was born on 5 July 1881 at Kaikoura, New Zealand, to Tom and Caroline Anne Cooke. Educated at Kaikoura Demonstration High School, he later moved to Wellington with his family. Like his father, Tom took up carpentry. On 4 June 1902 he married Maud Elizabeth Elliott. Cooke was an excellent band musician and was a first cornetist in the Wellington garrison band.

In 1912, with his wife and three children, he migrated to Australia and settled in Richmond, Victoria, where he worked as a builder. On 16 February 1915 he enlisted in the AIF and after a period of training at Broadmeadows and other camps was allotted as a reinforcement to the 24th Battalion. Cooke embarked for Egypt in November 1915 and was acting corporal from then until February 1916. He relinquished this rank on joining the 8th Battalion at Serapeum in the Suez Canal Zone on 24 February. This unit sailed for France on 26 March and from April to July served in the quiet sector of the western front near Armentières.

The 8th Battalion, with the rest of the 2nd Brigade, was in reserve when the 1st Australian Division took Pozières in the early morning of 24 July 1916. That night the 8th reinforced the attack and secured most of the remainder of the village. Early on the morning of the 25th the battalion completed the capture of Pozières, advancing northward beyond the village.

Despite counter-attacks and intense bombardment of their position, the 8th Battalion was able to retain its newly captured objectives. During this struggle Cooke was ordered, with his Lewis gun team, to a dangerous part of the line. Heavy enemy fire killed all his companions, but Cooke remained at his post firing his Lewis gun. When assistance finally reached this post Cooke was found dead beside his gun. He was one of eighty-one members of the battalion killed during the action.

Cooke's name is commemorated on the Australian War Memorial, Villers-Bretonneux. He was survived by his wife, who later remarried, and by his three children.

CURREY William Matthew

RANK   Private
UNIT   53rd Battalion, 14th Brigade, 5th Division
DATE   1 September 1918
PLACE Near Péronne, France

WILLIAM CURREY was born on 19 September 1895, at Wallsend, New South Wales, son of William Robert and Mary Ellen Currey. Educated at Dudley and Plattsburg public schools, he moved to Leichhardt, Sydney, and found employment as a wireworker. He had served for nearly two years with the 31st Infantry Regiment when the 1914–18 war began. Currey twice attempted to enlist without his parents' consent, giving a false age, but was discovered and discharged. When his parents gave their consent for his enlistment he was rejected on medical grounds and had to undergo surgery before being accepted for the AIF at Leichhardt on 9 October 1916. He was posted to the 4th Light Trench Mortar Battery, embarked for France in November and on 1 July 1917 was transferred to the 53rd Battalion. Later that year he fought at Polygon Wood, then returned to the Somme.

Currey was awarded the Victoria Cross for his part in the Australian attack at Péronne on 1 September 1918. The 53rd Battalion began taking heavy casualties early in the day, Currey's company in particular suffering from a 77 mm field gun firing at very close range. Despite heavy machine-gun fire Currey rushed forward and killed the whole crew and captured the weapon. Later, in the afternoon, the 53rd encountered intense fire from a strong point. Currey crept around the flank of the position and opened fire with a Lewis gun before rushing the post, inflicting many casualties and dispersing the survivors. His courageous action enabled the battalion attack to proceed. At 3 a.m. next morning he volunteered to warn an isolated company to withdraw: moving out into no man's land he stood up and called out to the company. This brought a hail of enemy fire down upon him. His respirator was punctured and he was gassed, but he succeeded in contacting the exposed company which then returned safely. By this stage of the battle, the 53rd was holding a line midway between Mont St Quentin and Péronne. By 10 a.m. other battalions of the 2nd and 5th Australian Divisions had forced the Germans out of both towns.

Despite his gassing Currey saw out the war with the 53rd Battalion, arriving back in Australia in January 1919; he was discharged on 2 April. In September he joined the New South Wales railways as a storeman and on 10 April the following year he married Emma Davies at Punchbowl. While employed with the railways he became active in the Australian Labor Party and on 16 May 1941 resigned from the railways to stand as Labor candidate for Kogarah in the Legislative Assembly. Currey won the seat and was twice re-elected, in 1944 and 1947, making the interests of ex-servicemen his particular concern. From 1930 until 1932 he served with the 45th Battalion in the militia, rising to warrant officer rank, and in 1940–41 with the Australian Instructional Corps. He also served at the German internment camp, Holdsworthy, for nearly a year.

Currey collapsed suddenly in Parliament House on 27 April 1948 and died three days later of coronary-vascular disease. He was survived by his wife and two daughters. He was cremated after a Presbyterian service. His ashes (and those of his wife, who died in 1974) are interred at Woronora cemetery. His name is commemorated on plaques at the Garden of Remembrance, Rookwood cemetery, and on the Leichhardt War Memorial. He is commemorated in the Jeffries–Currey Memorial Library, installed at the Dudley school in 1941 in memory of its two famous ex-pupils, and by a memorial park at Abermain, New South Wales.

His Victoria Cross and a portrait of him by John Longstaff are displayed in the Australian War Memorial's Hall of Valour.

DALZIEL Henry

RANK   Private
UNIT   15th Battalion, 4th Brigade, 4th Division
DATE   4 July 1918
PLACE Hamel Wood, France

'HARRY' DALZIEL was born on 18 February 1893 at Irvinebank, Qld, son of James and Eliza Maggie Dalziel. He was educated at Irvinebank and became a fireman with the Queensland Government Railways on the Cairns–Atherton route.

Dalziel enlisted in the AIF on 16 January 1915 and embarked with reinforcements for the 15th Battalion. He joined his unit at Gallipoli in July, served in the August battles and was eventually evacuated with his battalion to Egypt. On 31 May 1916 he embarked for France, going into the line at Bois Grenier and from July serving on the Somme, at Pozières and at Mouquet farm. In 1917 Dalziel saw action at Gueudecourt, Lagnicourt, Bullecourt and Messines before being wounded by shrapnel at Polygon Wood on 16 October. He resumed duty on 7 June 1918, first as a driver then as a gunner.

The actions for which Dalziel was awarded the Victoria Cross were performed during the battle of Hamel on 4 July 1918 when the 15th Battalion was given the task of capturing a position known as Pear trench. Artillery fire had been brought down on the trench but it had missed the protecting wire. The trench and its garrison were insufficiently damaged and the battalion's advance was halted by strong resistance. Dalziel, as second member of a Lewis gun team, helped his partner to counter enemy machine-gun fire. When fire opened up from another post he dashed forward and, with his revolver, killed or captured the crew and gun, thus allowing the advance to proceed. During this action the tip of his trigger-finger was shot away;

he was ordered to the rear, but continued to serve his gun in the final storming of Pear trench. Although again ordered back to the aid post, he continued to bring up ammunition which had been dropped by aeroplane, until he was shot in the head.

Dalziel's wound was so severe that his skull was smashed and the brain exposed. He required extensive medical treatment in Britain before he was able to return to Australia in January 1919. He received the Victoria Cross from King George V at Buckingham Palace on 13 December 1918. While travelling home by train, he received a hero's welcome at every station from Townsville to Atherton. He married Ida Maude Ramsay, a nurse who had served with the 17th Australian General Hospital, at South Brisbane on 8 April 1920. They took up a soldier settlement block, which they named 'Zenith', on the Tolga railway line. Because of Dalziel's injuries his wife assumed most of the day-to-day workload associated with running a small mixed farm.

Dalziel's interest in farming waned after a few years so he left his wife to run Zenith and moved south. He worked in a Sydney factory in the late 1920s, mined gold at Bathurst during the depression, and by 1933 had settled in Brisbane where he was unemployed for some time; he later received a war pension. In the early 1930s he joined the CMF, becoming a sergeant in the 9th/15th Battalion. He developed an interest in songwriting and some of his songs were published in Britain, including *A Song of the Table-land, The Old*

Sundowner and *Love Time, Merry Love Time.* He also attempted drawing, pottery and prose-writing. In 1956 he went to London for the Victoria Cross centenary celebrations and on 4 July laid a wreath on the cenotaph at Hamel.

Dalziel lived at Oxley, Queensland, prior to his death of a stroke on 24 July 1965 at the Repatriation General Hospital, Greenslopes, Brisbane. He was cremated with military honours. His name is commemorated by a plaque at Mt Thompson crematorium, Brisbane.

DARTNELL William Thomas
(alias **DARTNELL,** Wilbur Taylor)

RANK	Temporary Lieutenant
UNIT	25th (Service) Battalion (Frontiersmen), the Royal Fusiliers (City of London Regiment)
DATE	3 September 1915
PLACE	Near Maktau, British East Africa (now Kenya)

WILBUR DARTNELL was born at Collingwood, Melbourne, on 6 April 1885, to Henry and Rose Ann Dartnell. He was educated in Melbourne, became an actor, and was only fifteen years old when he enlisted in the 5th Contingent of the Victorian Mounted Rifles in February 1901. Dartnell served with this unit in South Africa from March 1901 until it left to return to Australia in March the following year.

He married Elizabeth Edith

Smyth at Queen Street, Melbourne, on 15 April 1907 and they settled at Fitzroy. In 1912 or 1913 he returned to South Africa and was in East London when war broke out in 1914. He worked for the Standard Printing Company and frequently contributed articles to their Saturday newspaper, the *Weekly Standard*.

Soon after the declaration of war Dartnell convened a meeting of Australians living in East London who were willing to proceed overseas on active service. As chairman of the meeting he placed his name at the head of the list and cabled the British War Office offering their services.

He left for Britain on 23 September and on 12 February 1915, using the name Wilbur Taylor Dartnell, joined the 25th (Service) Battalion (Frontiersmen), the Royal Fusiliers (City of London Regiment) as a temporary lieutenant. Initially he was stationed at Swaythling near Southampton whence he made trips to Belgium in charge of drafts of artillery horses.

In April 1915 Dartnell embarked for British East Africa with the Fusiliers and arrived in Mombasa on 6 May. They went at once to their post on the Uganda railway as their main task was to protect the railway from enemy raiding parties. From mid-June they were engaged in raids on Bukoba, the German base for attacks on the Ugandan frontier.

On 22 June at the battle of Bukoba, Dartnell led the attack and was the first man to enter the enemy's fort and haul down the German flag, for which he was mentioned in dispatches and recommended for the

Distinguished Service Order.

In August the battalion returned to British East Africa and established its headquarters at Voi with two of its companies stationed at Maktau to patrol the frontier. Dartnell, whose promotion to lieutenant had been confirmed on 25 July, was assigned on 1 September to a mounted infantry patrol. Two days later, near Maktau, his party was ambushed. In the subsequent fighting Dartnell was wounded in the leg and was being carried away when he realized that the badly wounded could not be removed. Believing that the enemy's African troops (askaris) killed the wounded, he insisted on being left behind in the hope of being able to save the lives of the other wounded men. Though he was twice asked to leave he ordered his men to abandon him and began firing on the Germans who were within twenty-five metres of his post. When his body was found seven enemy dead lay around it. He was awarded the Victoria Cross for giving his own life in a gallant attempt to save others. Dartnell was buried in Voi cemetery, Kenya. He was survived by his wife and a daughter.

The Victoria Cross was presented to Dartnell's widow by Sir Ronald Munro-Ferguson, Governor-General of Australia, at a private ceremony at Government House, Melbourne, on 7 October 1916. Dartnell's widow attended the Victoria Cross centenary celebrations in London in 1956. His Victoria Cross and other service medals were auctioned and then donated to the Australian War Memorial in 1984.

DAVEY Phillip

RANK   Corporal
UNIT   10th Battalion, 3rd
           Brigade, 1st Division
DATE   28 June 1918
PLACE   Merris, France

PHILLIP DAVEY was born at Goodwood, South Australia, on 10 October 1896, the son of William George and Elizabeth Davey. He was educated at Flinders Street Model School and Goodwood public school and was a horse driver when he enlisted in the AIF at Morphettville, Adelaide, on 22 December 1914. He embarked from Melbourne on 2 February 1915 and joined the 10th Battalion two weeks before the Anzac landing.

He contracted enteric fever on Gallipoli and following treatment was invalided to South Australia in January 1916. On 27 June 1916 he re-embarked with the 18th reinforcements, sailed to Britain, and rejoined the 10th on 3 October in the Ypres Salient. He was accidentally wounded on 15 March 1917 and gassed on 3 October; he had been appointed lance corporal on 9 May.

At Warneton, near Messines in Belgium, on 3 January 1918, Davey gained the Military Medal for crawling into no man's land under heavy fire to rescue a badly wounded comrade. His brothers Claude and Richard were also awarded Military Medals during the war.

Davey was promoted to corporal on 24 April 1918. He took part in a diversionary attack by the 10th Battalion on enemy positions at Merris, France, on 28 June. His platoon came under heavy fire and the commander was killed. Survivors were forced to shelter in a ditch under almost point-blank fire from a German machine-gun. Davey then single-handedly attacked the enemy gun with grenades, putting half the crew out of action. Running out of grenades, he returned to his own position for more. In his next attack he killed the remainder of the crew, which had been reinforced and numbered eight, and captured the gun. He then mounted the captured gun in a new position and, until he was wounded, efficiently used it to repel a determined counter-attack. For his bravery and initiative in this action he was awarded the Victoria Cross. Davey's wounds were so severe that he was invalided to hospital at Weymouth, UK. In September 1918 he was invested with his Victoria Cross by King George V at Buckingham Palace; on 19 October he embarked for Australia and was discharged in Adelaide on 24 February 1919.

After demobilization Davey joined the signal and telegraph branch of the South Australian Railways. He married Eugene Agnes Tomlinson on 25 August 1928; they had one daughter. Davey continued to work in Adelaide as a railway linesman. He suffered from emphysema and bronchitis for years before his death from a coronary occlusion at the Repatriation General Hospital, Springbank, South Australia, on 21 December 1953. He was buried with full military honours in the AIF Garden of Memorial Cemetery, West Terrace, Adelaide.

In 1967 Davey's medals were presented to the Australian War Memorial for inclusion in the then 'Victoria Cross Corner'; they are now displayed in the Hall of Valour.

DUNSTAN William

RANK	Corporal
UNIT	7th Battalion, 2nd Brigade, 1st Division
DATE	9 August 1915
PLACE	Lone Pine trenches, Gallipoli Peninsula, Turkey

WILLIAM DUNSTAN was born on 8 March 1895 at Ballarat East, Victoria, fourth child and third son of William John and Henrietta Dunstan. He was educated at Golden Point state school and left, aged fifteen, to join the clerical staff of Snows drapers at Ballarat. He joined the AMF under the compulsory service scheme in 1911 and gained the cadet rank of captain. He later transferred to the citizen forces as a lieutenant in the militia with the 70th Infantry (Ballarat Regiment).

On 2 June 1915 Dunstan enlisted in the AIF and a fortnight later embarked for Egypt as an acting sergeant of the 6th reinforcements of the 7th Battalion. With the 7th at Gallipoli he was twice mentioned in dispatches and three days before the Lone Pine attack was promoted to corporal. On 9 August, less than ten weeks after joining the AIF, he performed the deed for which he was awarded the Victoria Cross.

Early on the 9th the Turks made a determined counter-attack on a newly captured trench held by Lieutenant Tubb [q.v.], Corporals Burton [q.v.] and Dunstan and a few others. The Turks advanced up a sap and blew in the sandbag barricade but Dunstan, Tubb and Burton repulsed them and rebuilt it. Supported by strong bombing parties, the enemy twice more destroyed the barricade but were driven off and the barricade was rebuilt. A bomb burst between Dunstan and Burton, killing Burton and temporarily blinding Dunstan. Dunstan's wounds resulted in his return to Australia on 4 September and demobilization from the AIF on 1 February 1916. He rejoined the citizen forces, serving in the rank of area officer, Ballarat, and acting brigade major, 18th Infantry Brigade. He transferred to the 6th Infantry Battalion in Melbourne in 1921, the unattached list in 1923, and the reserve of officers in 1928. He retired with the rank of lieutenant.

Dunstan was presented with the Victoria Cross on 9 June 1916 by the Governor-General of Australia, Sir Ronald Munro-Ferguson, on the steps of Parliament House, Melbourne, amid an outburst of exceptional public fervour.

In November 1918 he married Marjorie Carnell, of Ballarat, at St Paul's Church of England, Ballarat East. There were two sons and a daughter, all of whom served in the 1939–45 war. Dunstan moved to Melbourne to take a position in the Repatriation Department and became private secretary to Sir Nicholas Lockyer, then acting secretary of the Department. In 1921 he joined the staff of the *Herald and Weekly Times* as an accountant. He was later promoted to the posts of chief accountant and assistant general manager and from 1934 until his retirement in 1953 was general manager and a world figure in the newspaper industry. His other interests included directorships of newsprint, radio and textile companies. He was joint manager of the Australian Newsprint Pool during the 1939–45 war and was, for fifteen years, chairman of the Australian Newspaper Proprietors' Association. He took a particular interest in Australian Newsprint Mills Ltd, the consortium which first planned to make newsprint from hardwood at New Norfolk, Tasmania.

Survived by his wife and children, Dunstan died suddenly of coronary vascular disease on 2 March 1957 and was cremated after a funeral service at Christ Church, South Yarra, attended by over 800 people including seven Victoria Cross winners. His ashes were interred at Springvale cemetery.

In October 1977 Dunstan's Victoria Cross was presented to the Australian War Memorial for inclusion in the Hall of Valour.

DWYER John James

RANK　　Sergeant
UNIT　　4th Machine Gun
　　　　Company, 4th Brigade,
　　　　4th Division
DATE　　26 September 1917
PLACE　　Zonnebeke, Belgium

JOHN DWYER was born at Lovett, Tasmania, on 9 March 1890, to Charles and Mary Dwyer. He lived with his parents at Alonnah, Bruny Island, and was educated at the state school there. Dwyer was working as a labourer in Queenstown when he enlisted on 4 February 1915. Posted to the 15th Battalion, Dwyer joined it in August on Gallipoli and remained with the 15th until March 1916. He then transferred to the 4th Machine Gun Company and went to France. Appointed lance corporal in December and promoted to temporary corporal then temporary sergeant, the following April, he was wounded on 9 June during the battle of Messines and lost his temporary rank until he rejoined the unit in August.

Dwyer earned his Victoria Cross during the battle of Polygon Wood when the 4th and 5th Australian Divisions attacked side by side on the southern edge of Zonnebeke. Dwyer, in charge of a Vickers machine-gun, had gone forward with the first wave of his brigade. When the final objective was reached Dwyer rushed his gun forward to obtain a commanding fire position. While he was advancing he noticed an enemy machine-gun causing casualties on the right flank. He rushed forward and fired his Vickers at the enemy, putting the gun out of action and killing the crew. He then seized the gun and established both it and his Vickers on the right flank of the brigade and inflicted further casualties during the subsequent counter-attack. The next day, when the position was heavily shelled, he carefully moved the gun to different positions and when the Vickers was put out of action by shell-fire he secured a reserve gun and very quickly had it operational.

He was appointed temporary regimental sergeant major in April 1918 and on 20 May was commissioned second lieutenant; three months later he was promoted to lieutenant.

On 23 January 1918 Dwyer received his Victoria Cross from King George V at Buckingham Palace. He returned to Australia in late August, and his AIF appointment ceased on 15 December. On 24 September 1919 Dwyer married Myrtle Dillon. They had six children. Early in the 1920s Dwyer became involved in local government and served as a councillor in the Bruny municipality from 1924 to 1926, before moving to New Norfolk where he established a sawmilling business.

In May 1931 Dwyer was elected to the Tasmanian House of Assembly as an ALP member for the seat of Franklin, and he held the seat until his death in 1962. He was Speaker of the House from 1942 to 1948, and Minister for Agriculture from 1948 until 1961 when he relinquished his portfolio for health reasons. He also served as deputy premier of Tasmania from 26 August 1958 to 12 May 1959. He died at Bruny Island, Tasmania, on 17 January 1962.

In 1956 Dwyer attended the Victoria Cross centenary in London and in 1959 his name was given to a club for army personnel at the Tasmania Command Ordnance Depot. His medals were presented to the Australian War Memorial in 1982 for inclusion in the Hall of Valour.

Three other members of the Dwyer family served in the AIF in the 1914–18 war.

GABY Alfred Edward

RANK   Lieutenant
UNIT   28th Battalion, 7th Brigade, 2nd Division
DATE   8 August 1918
PLACE   East of Villers-Bretonneux, France

ALFRED GABY was born on 25 January 1892 at Springfield, near Ringarooma, Tasmania, seventh son of Alfred and Adelaide Gaby. He was educated at Scottsdale and worked on his family's farm after leaving school. While working for his father he joined the militia and served for three years in the 12th Infantry Regiment (Launceston Regiment). At least two of his elder brothers had served in the South African war.

Before war broke out Gaby went to Katanning, Western Australia, where he worked as a labourer until his enlistment at Blackboy Hill Camp on 6 January 1916. He was posted to the 10th reinforcements to the 28th Battalion. Taken on strength on 6 August, Gaby was rapidly promoted because of his previous military service, and was made a sergeant on 30 December. On 7 April 1917 Gaby was appointed second lieutenant, and on 26 September lieutenant. A month later he was gassed in action.

At 4.20 a.m. on 8 August 1918, 2000 guns opened fire to commence the decisive battle of Amiens. Ludendorff would describe the defeat as *der Schwarze Tag* ('the black day') of the German army. Four Australian divisions were among the attacking troops with the 28th Battalion moving towards the first objective. Gaby, in command of Company D, moved with his unit to the east of Villers-Bretonneux towards Card Copse, where unbroken wire entanglements were encountered. Heavy fire from a German strong point covering a gap in the wire pinned down the Australians. Gaby found a gap in the wire and, single-handedly, approached an enemy strong point while machine-gun and rifle fire poured from it. He ran along the parapet, emptied his revolver into the garrison, drove the crews from their machine-guns and forced fifty of the enemy to surrender. This resulted in the capture of four machine-guns. He then reorganized his company and consolidated on the objective.

Three days later, on the morning of 11 August, during an attack east of Framerville, Gaby again led his company with great dash on to the objective. The Germans brought heavy rifle and machine-gun fire to bear upon the line and in the face of this fire Gaby walked along his line of posts encouraging his men to consolidate quickly. While engaged in this duty he was killed instantly by sniper fire.

He was awarded the Victoria Cross for his actions on 8 August and was buried in Heath cemetery, Harbonnières. He was unmarried.

His Victoria Cross is displayed in the Tasmanian Museum and Art Gallery, Hobart.

GORDON Bernard Sidney

RANK   Lance corporal
UNIT   41st Battalion, 11th Brigade, 3rd Division
DATE   27 August 1918
PLACE Fargny Wood, east of Bray, France

SIDNEY GORDON was born at Launceston, Tasmania, on 16 August 1891 to Charles and Mary Gordon. He was educated in Deloraine and

Devonport and was employed as a cooper's machinist at Beaconsfield. He later went to Townsville, Queensland, where he enlisted in the AIF on 27 September 1915. He served continuously with the 41st Battalion and was first wounded in France on 5 October 1917. He was appointed lance corporal in June 1918 and on 8 August earned the Military Medal for his conduct during an attack east of Hamel on the first day of the battle of Amiens. He single-handedly attacked a machine-gun crew which was holding up his section, killing the crew and capturing the gun. Later that day he stalked and killed an enemy sniper.

Eighteen days later, on the night of 26–27 August, Gordon won the Victoria Cross. The 41st Battalion attacked at 4.55 a.m., advancing the line past the bend in the Somme River. During the day the battalion was precariously wedged between the banks of the Somme and Fargny Wood. Gordon single-handedly attacked a German machine-gun post that was persistently enfilading the Australian position, killing the gunner and capturing the post, which consisted of one officer and ten men. He then entered Fargny Wood and cleared a trench, capturing twenty-nine prisoners and two machine-guns. He took over further trenches, capturing twenty-two prisoners and three machine-guns. The company that Gordon had assisted, using its own mortars and machine-guns, then moved on its objective; by 8.05 a.m. on the 27th the battalion had consolidated after a hard fought advance of over 1000 metres.

In another advance, on 1 September, in the Mont St Quentin area, Gordon was wounded.

He returned to Australia in January 1919, was demobilized in April, and after a period as a grocer at Clayfield, Queensland, took up a dairy farming property near Beaudesert. Gordon married Caroline Edith Manley, née Victorsen, a widow, on 7 September 1938 at Ann Street Presbyterian Church, Brisbane, and they had a family of two sons and one daughter. Gordon had married Evelyn Catherine Lonergan on 29 December 1915 at Launceston, with Catholic rites; there were six children of this marriage.

During the 1939–45 war Gordon served in the Queensland 31st Battalion (the Kennedy Regiment). He visited London in 1956 for the Victoria Cross centenary. He lived at Torquay, Queensland, prior to his death there on 19 October 1963 at the age of seventy-two. His ashes were interred at Mt Thompson crematorium.

In January 1960 the Gordon Soldiers' Club was opened at the 101st Wireless Regiment Headquarters, Cabarlah, near Toowoomba, Queensland. One of the machine-guns captured by Gordon is displayed in the Australian War Memorial's Hall of Valour.

GRIEVE Robert Cuthbert

RANK   Captain
UNIT   37th Battalion, 10th
           Brigade, 3rd Division
DATE   7 June 1917
PLACE   Messines, Belgium

BOB GRIEVE was born at Brighton, Melbourne, on 19 June 1889, the son of John and Annie Deas Grieve. Educated at the Caulfield Grammar School and Wesley College, Melbourne, he became an interstate commercial traveller in soft goods upon leaving school. Grieve was a keen footballer and cricketer and had nine months' service in the Victorian Rangers. Enlisting on 9 June 1915 as a private, he was commissioned second lieutenant on 17 January 1916 in the 37th Battalion, and promotion to lieutenant came on 1 May, a month before the 37th embarked. His division trained in Britain before moving to France in November. On 9 April 1917, after three months secondment to the 10th Light Trench Mortar Battery, Grieve was promoted to captain and given command of A Company.

Two months later the 3rd Division fought its first major battle at Messines on 7 June; it was the southernmost of nine attacking British divisions. Fire came from a pillbox just as Grieve's company was going through a gap in the wire. Almost immediately half the men and all the officers, except Grieve, were struck down. Grieve spotted the hostile pillbox and, after failing to obtain Stokes mortar and Vickers machine-gun support, took a bag of Mills bombs and, throwing as he advanced, rushed from shell-hole to shell-hole under cover of the dust from the bomb bursts. He got through the pillbox's arc of fire and into the trench. Here he encountered the German garrison sheltering from the allied barrage. He threw one bomb close to the pillbox, which stopped the gunners' fire. He then rolled two more bombs through the firing slit, killing all of the occupants. He called his company forward and they soon occupied the trench, but Grieve was sniped and badly wounded in the right shoulder as he signalled part of the line to come up on the flank.

His wound kept him hospitalized in Britain for six months; he rejoined his unit in France but became seriously ill with acute trench nephritis and double pneumonia, which necessitated further treatment in Britain. He was returned medically unfit to Australia in May 1918 and his AIF appointment was terminated on 28 June. On 7 August he married May Isobel Bowman, a sister in the Australian Army Nursing Service who had nursed him, at Scots Church, Sydney.

As there had been no officers of the company left to initiate the recommendation for Grieve's Victoria Cross, eyewitnesses from the ranks furnished the details. It was the first Victoria Cross won by the 3rd Division and Grieve received it from the King at Buckingham Palace on 20 October 1917.

He returned to the soft goods trade and founded the firm of Grieve, Gardner & Co. in Melbourne, which he ran until he collapsed in his office and died of cardiac failure on 4 October 1957. He was buried in the Presbyterian section, Springvale cemetery. His wife had died in 1929 and they had no children. While he was a patient at Heidelberg Repatriation Hospital he was presented to the Queen during her visit in 1954. He had served as a captain of the 4th Battalion of the Victorian Volunteer Defence Corps from June 1942 until his retirement on 18 September 1944.

Grieve's Victoria Cross was presented to Wesley College, Melbourne, where it is now displayed.

HALL Arthur Charles

RANK	Corporal
UNIT	54th Battalion, 14th Brigade, 5th Division
DATE	1–2 September 1918
PLACE	Péronne, France

ARTHUR HALL was born at Granville, New South Wales, on 11 August 1896, the son of Charles and Emma Jane Hall. His father owned Glenelg and Willeroon stations in the Nyngan district of northern New South Wales and, after receiving his education at All Saints' College, Bathurst, where he served in the school cadets, Arthur became an overseer on these properties. He enlisted in the AIF at Dubbo on 3 April 1916 and was allotted to the 6th reinforcements to the 54th Battalion. He joined it on 8 February 1917.

Hall was wounded in the leg on 30 March but returned to his unit on 21 April; he was promoted to lance corporal in June and corporal in October. It was for his bravery, brilliant leadership and devotion to duty during the operations at Péronne, 1–2 September 1918, that he was awarded the Victoria Cross. During the attack on 1 September, Hall single-handedly rushed a machine-gun post which was checking the advance, killing four of the occupants and capturing fifteen others and two machine-guns. He then crossed the objective with a small party and covered the advance of the rest of his company. Advancing ahead of the main party, he located, assaulted and captured many small parties of men and machine-guns. At one stage he was able to report that the recently destroyed bridge over the Péronne moat was unguarded and his unit was able to cross nearby on planks and debris.

Next day the 54th continued to clear Péronne of enemy. During a heavy barrage Hall carried a wounded comrade, who was urgently in need of medical attention, to safety.

On 12 October, the 54th Battalion disbanded and Hall joined the 56th Battalion. He was decorated by King George V at Buckingham Palace on 10 April 1919 and was temporary sergeant from 6 March until his return to Australia on 8 May. He was discharged in Sydney on 3 August. He resumed his occupation as a pastoralist and, during the 1939–45 war, was commissioned and served as a lieutenant in the 5th Garrison Battalion from 1939 until 1943. Hall was placed on the retired list on 16 November 1943 after a short period of service with the 7th Garrison Battalion.

Hall married Catherine Jessie Hemington Harris on 26 April 1927, and they had three sons and a daughter. He worked his property, Gundooee, in the Coolabah district of New South Wales prior to his death at Nyngan on 25 February 1978. He was survived by his wife and four children. He was buried at the tiny Anglican church of St Matthew's, West Bogan, which had been built from timber cut and milled on his property.

Hall's Victoria Cross is now on display in the Hall of Valour at the Australian War Memorial.

HAMILTON John (Patrick)

RANK   Private
UNIT   3rd Battalion, 1st
           Brigade, 1st Division
DATE   9 August 1915
PLACE   Lone Pine trenches,
           Gallipoli Peninsula,
           Turkey

JOHN HAMILTON was born at Orange, New South Wales, on 24 January 1896 to William and Catherine Hamilton. He worked for his father, a butcher, in Penshurst and served in the militia before enlisting on 15 September 1914. He joined the newly raised 3rd Battalion and embarked for Egypt with that unit on 18 October. He took part in the original landing on 25 April 1915 and a month later was evacuated with influenza. He did not resume duty until 2 June. It was during the furious fighting at Lone Pine on 9 August that Hamilton earned his Victoria Cross.

The Turks had launched a violent general attack extending along much of the front. The northern part of the assault was directed at the junction of the 3rd and 4th Battalions. At Sasse's sap the enemy forced the Australians back but were ousted by a counter-attack. Later the enemy forced the barricade and streamed up the sap towards the 3rd Battalion headquarters. The adjutant of the 3rd Battalion instructed several men to get out on the parapet and attack the Turks in the trench and those coming across open ground. Hamilton, under the cover of a few sandbags, lay out in the open shouting to those in the trenches where best to land their bombs while he kept up constant sniping fire against the Turkish bomb throwers. His example had much to do with the enemy being driven off during this attack.

On 3 May 1916, after the unit had moved to France, Hamilton was promoted to corporal and about a year later to sergeant. From 5 July 1918 he was a student at No.5 Officer Cadet Battalion, Cambridge, UK; he graduated second lieutenant on 2 January 1919 and was allotted as a general reinforcement officer; he was promoted to lieutenant on 2 April that same year. He returned to the depleted 3rd Battalion on 22 April 1919, and went back to Australia on 6 July to live at Tempe, Sydney, after demobilization on 12 September. He worked for many years as a waterside worker, and also as a shipping clerk and storeman and packer. He was an active member of the Waterside Workers' Federation.

Hamilton returned to the active

list as a lieutenant on 3 June 1940 and was posted to the 16th Garrison Battalion, with which he served until September 1942. He went to New Guinea with the 3rd Pioneer Battalion, then served with Australian employment companies until 1944 when he transferred to the army's Labour Service. With this unit he served on Bougainville from July 1945 until April 1946. He had been promoted to captain on 21 October 1944. His AIF appointment was terminated on 19 August 1946.

Hamilton died of cerebro-vascular disease at Concord Repatriation Hospital on 27 February 1961. After a private funeral he was buried in the Church of England section of Woronora cemetery. He was survived by his wife Myrtle, who died in 1975, and his only son.

HOWELL George Julian

RANK   Corporal
UNIT   1st Battalion, 1st Brigade, 1st Division
DATE   6 May 1917
PLACE   Bullecourt, France

'SNOWY' HOWELL was born at Enfield, New South Wales, on 19 November 1893, to Francis John and Martha Howell. Educated at the Croydon Park and Burwood public schools, he took up bricklaying and later became a builder in the Enfield area of Sydney. He enlisted on 3 June 1915 and was posted as a reinforcement to the 1st Battalion, which he joined on Gallipoli on 1 November. Howell went with the 1st to France and was wounded in July 1916 during the battle of Pozières; he was appointed lance corporal on 10 December and promoted to corporal on 6 February 1917.

On 9 April Howell was awarded the Military Medal for courage and devotion to duty while leading a rifle bombing section during the 1st Battalion's capture of the village of Demicourt.

Fourteen divisions, including the 2nd Australian Division, attacked the Hindenburg line on 3 May 1917. Only the Canadians on the extreme right and the 6th Australian Brigade on the extreme left were able to take and hold their objectives. In the next few days more troops were drawn in to hold and extend the gains of 3 May. When the Germans launched a general counter-attack on 6 May they used flame-throwers, which caused the 3rd Brigade to withdraw from its trenches. At 6 a.m. Howell notified battalion headquarters that the battalion to his right was retiring. The 1st Battalion commander then hurriedly organized a group to resist the enemy assault and a fierce bombing fight ensued. Howell, fearing that the enemy would outflank his battalion, climbed on to the top of the parapet and bombed the enemy, forcing them back along the trench. When his bombs ran out Howell continued to pursue the enemy with his bayonet but as he was exposed to heavy bomb and rifle fire it was not long before he was severely wounded. In the interval, the retreating battalions rallied and a party from the 1st succeeded in reclaiming the ground lost to the enemy earlier. Howell received both the Victoria Cross and Military Medal from King George V at Buckingham Palace on 21 July 1917.

Howell's multiple wounds necessitated prolonged hospital treatment and he was returned to Australia in October 1917 and discharged on 5 June 1918. On 1 March 1919 he married a nurse, Sadie Lillian Yates, at St Stephen's Presbyterian Church, Sydney, and they settled at Coogee. He then joined the advertising staff of Smiths Newspapers and later worked for the Bulletin Newspaper Company. By 1933 he was New South Wales representative for the *Standard,* Brisbane, and the *Queensland Worker.*

During the 1939–45 war Howell served as an army staff sergeant at Eastern Command Headquarters, Paddington. In August 1944 he joined the United States Sea Transport Service and was thus able to participate in the invasion of Leyte at the commencement of the Philippines campaign.

In December 1953 Howell moved from Sydney to Western Australia, and settled in Applecross, a suburb of Perth. He then moved to Gunyidi, via Watheroo, and died at the Repatriation General Hospital, Perth, on 24 December 1964. He was cremated at Karrakatta crematorium and a plaque was placed in the Western Australian Garden of Remembrance. A soldier's club bearing his name was opened at Randwick. He had visited London for the Victoria Cross centenary celebrations in 1956.

INGRAM George Mawby (Morby)

RANK	Lieutenant
UNIT	24th Battalion, 6th Brigade, 2nd Division
DATE	5 October 1918
PLACE	Montbrehain, east of Péronne, France

GEORGE INGRAM was born at Bendigo, Victoria, on 18 March 1889, to George Ronald and Charlotte Ingram. He was educated at Lilydale state school and at fourteen joined the militia. He was attached to No. 7 Company of the Australian Garrison Artillery; he attended an exhibition in New Zealand in 1906 as a member of an Australian military contingent. When Ingram completed his apprenticeship as a carpenter and joiner he moved to Caulfield, Victoria, and set up business as a building contractor. On 19 January 1910, at East Prahran, he married Jane Francis Nichols in a Congregational ceremony. There were no children of the marriage, which was dissolved in 1926 with Ingram as petitioner, the grounds being desertion by his wife.

Ingram enlisted on 10 December 1914 with the 3rd Battalion, Australian Naval and Military Expeditionary Force, and served in New Guinea until, as a corporal, he was discharged on 19 January 1916. That same day he enlisted in the AIF and was allotted to the 16th reinforcements to the 24th Battalion which he joined in France early in January 1917 with the rank of acting corporal. He relinquished the rank in the unit but by 18 March had progressed to temporary sergeant. In March, during the German withdrawal to the Hindenburg line, Ingram was awarded the Military Medal near Bapaume for great courage and initiative as a member of a bombing section and, in particular, for his excellent placement of bombs. He fell ill and was hospitalized in Britain and it was not until June that he rejoined his unit. In September he was sent to hospital again and when he rejoined his unit on 10 October he was made company sergeant major.

Ingram was gazetted second lieutenant on 20 June 1918 but three days later was again in hospital and unable to resume duty until 12 July. He overcame his illnesses and was with his unit during the allied offensives of 1918. He was promoted to lieutenant on 24 October.

It was during the 24th's last major battle at Montbrehain, east of Péronne, that Ingram won his Victoria Cross. The previous day the battalion had helped capture the Beaurevoir sector and it was expecting to rest, but it was hurriedly organized to attack more strongly defended German positions. Early on the 5th, at about 6 a.m., the advance began and it was not long before strong points and machine-gun nests were encountered. B Company, of which Ingram was a member, had a difficult advance hampered by snipers and machine-gun fire. Ingram led his platoon against one strong point and the platoon succeeded, after a fierce fight, in capturing nine machine-guns and killing forty-two enemy. When his company commander was wounded Ingram organized and led a charge against an old quarry which was defended by forty machine-guns and over a hundred men. He alone rushed the first post and shot six enemy and captured a machine-gun. On two subsequent occasions he displayed great dash and resourcefulness in capturing enemy posts, inflicting many casualties and taking sixty-two prisoners. On the last assault he captured over thirty Germans in a cellar after shooting the gunner who had been firing through the cellar ventilator.

The fight for Montbrehain raged all day and it was not until 8 p.m. that the line on the objective was linked up and consolidated. The capture of Montbrehain was a brilliant but expensive victory and was the last action fought by Australian infantry during the 1914–18 war.

Ingram was decorated by King George V at Buckingham Palace on 15 February 1919 and in April returned to Australia. His AIF appointment was terminated on 2 June. He became general foreman with E.A. & Frank Watts Pty Ltd, building contractors. He was one of the permanent guards for the Shrine of Remembrance in Melbourne from 1935 to 1944. He saw further service in the 1939–45 war when he rose to the rank of captain in the Royal Australian Engineers. He was placed on the retired list on 6 May 1944.

Ingram married a widow, Lillian Wakeling, née Hart, on 10 February 1927 at the Methodist parsonage, Malvern. She died in May 1951 and he married another widow, Myrtle Lydia Thomas, née Cornell, on 24 December at Brunswick Methodist Church. Ingram attended the Victoria Cross centenary in London in 1956 and died at his home at Hastings, Victoria, on 1 July 1961. He was buried in the Methodist section of Frankston cemetery. He was survived by his third wife, Myrtle Lydia Thomas, and their son, and a son from his second marriage.

INWOOD Reginald Roy

RANK Private
UNIT 10th Battalion, 3rd
Brigade, 1st Division
DATE 20–21 September 1917
PLACE Polygon Wood, east of
Ypres, Belgium

ROY INWOOD was born at North Adelaide, South Australia, on 14 July 1890, eldest son of Edward and Mary Ann Inwood. Educated at North Adelaide public school and Broken Hill Model School, he worked as a miner prior to enlisting in the AIF on 24 August 1914. He was one of three brothers who served in the AIF: Robert was killed at Pozières on 24 July 1916 and Harold was wounded in France and returned to Australia in November 1917. Inwood was sent to Morphettville with the 10th Battalion quota from Broken Hill and he embarked on 20 October and served at Gallipoli, where he was appointed lance corporal in August 1915. By April

1916 the battalion had moved to France. Inwood, who had been promoted to temporary corporal in August, was in October reduced to private for having been absent without leave.

It was during the battle of Menin Road, when the 10th attacked at Polygon Wood on the morning of 20 September 1917, that Roy Inwood won the Victoria Cross. The 3rd Brigade advanced with the 11th Battalion taking the first objective, the 12th taking the second, and the 9th and 10th Battalions moving through to take the third. At this stage Inwood went out alone to an enemy strong point and captured it after taking nine prisoners and killing several of the enemy, allowing the advance to continue until the third objective was gained. The battalion then consolidated its posts and wired its front before beating off enemy counter-attacks. It was expected that the enemy would group for a counter-attack that evening so Inwood volunteered to go out in the dark, 600 metres in front of his line, to report on enemy movements. The attack did not eventuate. Next morning Inwood and a member of the 7th Battalion located a machine-gun which was causing casualties. They crept up behind it and bombed it so effectively that only one gunner survived; he was taken prisoner and forced to carry his gun back to the Australian lines.

After Polygon Wood Inwood was appointed lance corporal on 28 September, and promoted to corporal on 17 October, then sergeant, before he left the battalion on 30 May 1918. He returned to Australia on 24 August and was demobilized on 12 December 1918. He returned to a hero's welcome in Broken Hill which he publicly contrasted to the jeering he had received when he left Broken Hill as a recruit. Broken Hill was not a comfortable place for Inwood as he was accused by the local MHR of trying to incite trouble between returned soldiers and the working class. He soon moved to Adelaide and on 31 December 1918 married a widow, Mabel Alice Collins, née Weber. They divorced in 1921.

In 1927 he married Evelyn Owens; there were no children. In 1942, as a widower, he married Louise Gates. From 1928 he worked as an attendant with the Adelaide City Council, retiring in 1955, and in 1956 went to London for the Victoria Cross centenary celebrations. During the 1939–45 war he had served as a warrant officer with the Australian Military Forces. He lived at Norwood, South Australia, and later Tara Private Hospital, St Peters, where he died on 23 October 1971. He was accorded a full military funeral and was buried in the AIF cemetery, West Terrace, Adelaide, on 27 October.

Inwood left his Victoria Cross to the 10th Battalion Ex-Servicemen's Association, who presented it to the Corporation of the City of Adelaide on 19 September 1972. It is displayed in the council chamber. The Other Ranks Mess, 10th Battalion, Torrens Parade Ground, Adelaide, is called the Roy Inwood Club.

JACKA Albert

RANK	Lance Corporal
UNIT	14th Battalion, 4th Brigade, New Zealand and Australian Division
DATE	19–20 May 1915
PLACE	Courtney's Post, Gallipoli Peninsula, Turkey

ALBERT JACKA was born on 10 January 1893 at Winchelsea, Victoria, one of seven children of Nathaniel and Elizabeth Jacka. His family moved to Wedderburn when he was five and he went to school there and obtained his standard and merit certificates. His father worked in the timber industry, first supplying sleepers to the Victorian Railways, and later timber to the mines in Bendigo. On leaving school Albert went to work for his father and for a short time was an engine-cleaner at Bendigo. At the age of eighteen he obtained employment with the Victorian State Forests Department and was subsequently stationed at Wedderburn, Cohuna, Koondrook, Lake Charm and Heathcote.

Jacka enlisted in the AIF at Heathcote on 8 September 1914 but as his papers were lost he had to do so again in Melbourne ten days later. His unit embarked on 22 December and spent two months training before landing at Anzac Cove, Gallipoli, on 26 April 1915.

On 19 May, the Turks launched a general attack to push the Australians into the sea. They seized ten metres of trench at Courtney's Post, but Australians at either end stopped them from continuing to advance. At the northern end Jacka, with several others, tried to evict the Turks, but was beaten back. It was then decided that while a feint was made from the same end, Jacka would attack from the rear. The party waited long enough for Jacka to circle to the rear and then threw two bombs and gave covering fire. Jacka leapt over the parapet, shot five Turks with his rifle, bayonetted two others and forced the rest to flee the captured trench. He was awarded the Victoria Cross for this action and received it from King George V at Windsor Castle on 29 September 1916. It was the first Victoria Cross to be awarded to the AIF in the 1914–18 war.

Jacka was appointed lance corporal on 27 August 1915, the following day was promoted to corporal, and on 12 September to sergeant. On 14 November he became a company sergeant major and second lieutenant on 29 April 1916. He was promoted to lieutenant on 18 August and his final promotion, to captain, came on 15 March 1917.

At Pozières, on 7 August 1916, the Germans overran a portion of the line which included Jacka's dug-out. He charged a large number of enemy who were rounding up prisoners and a furious close quarter fight ensued in which he was wounded three times, once through the neck. Inspired by Jacka, the captured men turned on their captors: many Germans were taken prisoner and the line was retaken. For his actions Jacka received the Military Cross. C.E.W. Bean wrote of this day that Jacka's counter-attack 'stands as the most dramatic and effective act of individual audacity in the history of the AIF'. At Bullecourt, on 8 April 1917, when the 4th Division was preparing to attack the Hindenburg line, Jacka, then intelligence officer of the 14th, made a dangerous night reconnaissance of the wire in front of the objective. He got through the wire in two places, brought back a report, and then went out to lay tapes on the assault line. As he was doing so, two Germans approached. He attempted to fire his revolver as they came at him, but nothing happened. Jacka rushed them, seizing the officer first, and eventually brought both in as prisoners. The attacking Australian troops then assembled unseen on the tapes and Jacka's action undoubtedly saved them from bombardment and heavy fire. For this he received a bar to the Military Cross. There has been speculation as to whether Jacka merited two bars to his Victoria Cross. C.E.W. Bean wrote: 'Everyone who knows the facts, knows that Jacka earned the Victoria Cross three times'.

On other occasions Jacka exhibited considerable military skill. At Messines he made a valuable reconnaissance and led his company in taking 800 metres of territory and capturing a field gun. At Polygon Wood, just after Jacka had returned from Britain where he was sent to recover from a wound he had received in July 1917, he was virtually responsible for controlling the 14th, which had for some time been known as 'Jacka's Mob'.

At the end of May 1918 Jacka was badly gassed and a missile passed through his trachea. He was evacuated to No. 20 Casualty Clearing Station at Vignacourt and it was thought for a time that he would not recover. When he did he was sent to Britain for two operations and a long recuperative period. He returned to Australia on 6 September 1919 and his AIF appointment ended on 10 January 1920 when he returned to Melbourne to a hero's welcome.

Jacka entered business with two former members of the 14th Battalion and helped establish a merchant and importing firm, but the business collapsed during the depression. He married Veronica Carey in 1929, and was elected to the St Kilda Council. He later became mayor, and displayed great concern for the welfare of the unemployed in his municipality.

His war wounds, business pressures and the worries of office all contributed to his breakdown in health. On 18 December 1931 he entered Caulfield Repatriation Hospital and a month later, on 17 January 1932, died of chronic nephritis; he was buried with full military honours in St Kilda cemetery on the 19th. He had eight Victoria Cross winners as pallbearers. A memorial stone, with a bas-relief portrait of Jacka by sculptor Wallace Anderson, was erected over his grave on 15 May and a house was purchased for his widow from public subscription.

He was survived by his wife and his adopted daughter, Betty, and predeceased his parents.

His name is commemorated on a plaque at the Victorian Garden of Remembrance, Springvale war cemetery, and by a number of streets in Melbourne and Canberra. In 1982 the St Kilda City Council renamed parts of the busy Lower Esplanade and Marine Parade as Jacka Boulevard. For many years the 14th Battalion commemorated the anniversary of his death with a memorial service at his grave and this is being continued by the St Kilda Council and the St Kilda Historical Society. A portrait by George Coates is displayed in the Hall of Valour at the Australian War Memorial.

JACKSON John William Alexander

RANK	Private
UNIT	17th Battalion, 5th Brigade, 2nd Division
DATE	25–26 June 1916
PLACE	South-east of Bois Grenier, near Armentières, France

WILLY JACKSON was born on 13 September 1897 at Gunbar, near Hay, New South Wales, to John and Adelaide Ann Jackson. He was educated at and then lived and worked with his parents on a property at Merriwa.

He enlisted on 20 February 1915 and was posted to the 17th Battalion, with which he embarked in May. After training at Heliopolis, Egypt, he landed on Gallipoli on 20 August. After the evacuation in December, the 17th manned outposts in the Sinai desert until early March 1916 when it embarked for France as part of the 2nd Division. On 7 April the division took over forward positions in the quiet Armentières sector. As a prelude to the battle of the Somme an order was issued that as many raids as possible were to be carried out between 20 and 30 June. It was during one of these raids that Jackson became the youngest Australian to win the Victoria Cross; his award was also the first won on the western front by an Australian and the first won by the 2nd Australian Division.

On the night of 25–26 June Jackson was one of eighty-two Australian raiders who entered the German trenches. Engineers with the party blew up two bomb stores and five minutes later the party withdrew after causing considerable havoc, but as they crossed no man's land they suffered casualties from enemy artillery fire. Jackson got back to his lines safely, handed over a prisoner, and immediately went back out into the heavy shell-fire to assist in bringing in one of the thirteen wounded. He went out again and was assisting a sergeant to bring in another wounded man when his arm was nearly blown off and the sergeant was knocked unconscious. Despite his terrible wounds Jackson returned to his lines and got assistance, then went out again to search for the sergeant and the wounded man he had been helping in. One of the men was located and escorted to safety and Jackson was then dispatched for treatment. His arm was amputated. He spent a long period in hospital and in May 1917 was invalided to Australia, and discharged on 15 September. Jackson was first recommended for the Distinguished

Conduct Medal before a recommendation for the Victoria Cross was submitted. The original recommendation was not withdrawn and was in fact approved two weeks after the award of the Victoria Cross. The Distinguished Conduct Medal was subsequently cancelled by an announcement in the *London Gazette* of 20 October 1916.

Jackson became a hotel-keeper at Wollongong for eighteen months or so after his discharge. Then he took up a property in his home district, Merriwa, but was dogged by six droughts in seven years. When the depression came Jackson left the land for Sydney in search of employment and in the years that followed had several jobs, including a greengrocery business and a position as a clerk with the Metropolitan Water Sewerage and Drainage Board. He married Ivy Muriel Alma Morris at St Paul's Anglican Church, Kogarah, on 17 January 1931. There was one child of the marriage which was dissolved in 1955. During the 1939–45 war Jackson served as an acting sergeant in Eastern Command Provost Company from 1941 until 1942. In October 1946 he was seriously injured in a motor accident and in 1953 he moved to Melbourne. He was appointed commissionnaire and inquiry attendant of the Melbourne City Council at the Melbourne Town Hall. He visited London in 1956 for the Victoria Cross centenary, and was still employed by the city council when he died at the Repatriation General Hospital, Heidelberg, of arteriosclerotic heart disease on 5 August 1959.

He was cremated and his ashes interred in the Boronia Gardens, Springvale cemetery.

JEFFRIES Clarence Smith

RANK   Captain
UNIT   34th Battalion, 9th Brigade, 3rd Division
DATE   12 October 1917
PLACE   Passchendaele, Belgium

'JEFF' JEFFRIES was born at Wallsend, New South Wales, on 26 October 1894, the son of Joshua and Barbara Jeffries. He was educated at Dudley primary school and Newcastle collegiate and high schools and became a mining surveyor at Abermain Collieries on the state's northern coalfields, where his father was general manager. Jeffries was in charge of the survey department of Abermain Collieries, and had had considerable previous militia experience in the 14th (Hunter River) Infantry when he was called up for training at the outbreak of war. On 1 February 1916 he was appointed to the AIF with the rank of second lieutenant, was posted to the 34th Battalion and embarked from Australia on 27 May. During the 3rd Division's training period he was gazetted lieutenant as from 1 August. Wounded in the thigh during the battle of Messines on 9 June 1917, he completely recovered and was able to rejoin his unit in September. He had been promoted to captain and company commander on 26 June 1917.

It was during the latter stages of the third battle of Ypres, which had commenced on 31 July 1917, that Jeffries won the Victoria Cross. After the three successful step-by-step battles that culminated in the victory at Broodseinde on 4 October, the weather closed in. The British attack on the 9 October, the first battle of Passchendaele, was unsuccessful and the Australians were brought back into the line to fight the second battle of Passchendaele on 12 October. The attacks of the 3rd and 4th Australian Divisions, with the New Zealand and British divisions, were beaten back by the Germans and it was not until 6 November that the Canadian Corps, which relieved the Australians, finally captured Passchendaele.

In the 34th's advance on 12 October the first point of resistance encountered was two pillboxes east of Augustus Wood. Jeffries organized a bombing party and rushed one emplacement, capturing two machine-guns and twenty-five prisoners. He then led his company forward under heavy artillery and machine-gun fire to the objective. As the 34th prepared for the next stage of the advance it was harassed by machine-gun fire. Jeffries gathered another party of twelve men, and although he was killed in the attack, the group successfully captured two guns and thirty more prisoners. The unit's advance to the second objective continued but every officer of the unit was either killed or wounded before it was completed. The 9th Brigade took the second objective but did not have enough men or supplies to hold the position and was ordered to withdraw during the afternoon.

Jeffries was buried in Tyne Cot cemetery, near Passchendaele. In 1947 the people of Abermain established a memorial park in his honour and his name was linked with that of William Currey, another Victoria Cross winner, in the Jeffries–Currey Memorial Library at the Dudley primary school, Newcastle. When his mother died in 1954 Jeffries's Victoria Cross was bequeathed to the Warriors' Chapel of Christchurch Cathedral, Newcastle.

JENSEN Joergen Christian

RANK	Private
UNIT	50th Battalion, 13th Brigade, 4th Division
DATE	2 April 1917
PLACE	Noreuil, France

JOERGEN JENSEN was born at Loegstoer, Denmark, on 15 January 1891, to Joergen Christian and Christiane Jensen. He migrated to Australia in March 1909, having spent the previous year in Britain. After disembarking in Melbourne he worked as a labourer at Margan and Port Pirie, South Australia, and was naturalized on 7 September 1914 in Adelaide.

Stating his occupation as labourer, he enlisted in Adelaide on 23 March 1915, and was posted as a reinforcement to the 10th Battalion, then on Gallipoli, which he joined on 28 September. After the evacuation, in February 1916, nearly 500 members of the 10th were transferred to form the 50th Battalion. Jensen went to France with the 10th, was wounded in August, and upon recovery he too was transferred to the 50th in January 1917.

At 5.30 a.m. on 2 April the 50th and 51st Battalions attacked the German 'outpost village' of Noreuil, which was one of a string of villages fringing the Hindenburg line. Part of the 50th's assaulting force penetrated and enveloped the enemy positions, silencing them with rifle grenades and bombs. On the right, however, the advance was temporarily checked by a barricade which Stokes mortars had failed to dislodge. A bombing party was sent to deal with the enemy post which consisted of a machine-gun and forty-five men. One of the party, a Private O'Connor, sniped at and killed the gunner at the post, enabling Jensen to get close enough to throw in his first bomb. Jensen still had one bomb in his hand and he pulled the pin out of another with his teeth. He bluffed the enemy with the two bombs and told them that they were surrounded, thus inducing them to surrender. He sent one of his prisoners to order a neighbouring party to surrender, which they did. When some Australians fired on the latter party, Jensen stood up on the barricade, waved his helmet until the fire ceased and then sent his prisoners back to the Australian lines. Noreuil was taken later in the day after a fierce fight.

Two days after his Victoria Cross exploit Jensen was appointed lance corporal, three months later was promoted to corporal and on 5 October was promoted to temporary sergeant. King George V presented the

Victoria Cross to Jensen at Buckingham Palace on 21 July 1917. Jensen then served from July to October with the 13th Training Battalion and returned to the 50th on 6 October. He was severely wounded at Villers-Bretonneux on 5 May 1918, which necessitated long hospitalization. Jensen returned to Australia on 24 August and was discharged on 12 December 1918 in Adelaide, where he worked for a time as a bottle-oh. He lived in St Peters until his death on 31 May 1922. He had married a divorcée, Katy Herman, née Arthur, at the Adelaide Registry Office on 13 July 1921. She later remarried.

Jensen was buried in the AIF section of the West Terrace cemetery, Adelaide.

JOYNT William Donovan

RANK Lieutenant
UNIT 8th Battalion, 2nd Brigade, 1st Division
DATE 23 August 1918
PLACE Herleville Wood, near Chuignes, France

WILLIAM JOYNT was born at Elsternwick, Victoria, on 19 March 1889, to Edward and Alice Joynt. He was educated at The Grange, Toorak, and Melbourne Grammar School, then studied accountancy until he was twenty. Joynt then became a pastoralist and travelled extensively in northern and western Australia to gain experience in sheep and cattle farming as well as wheat farming in the Mallee, Victoria.

He left a farming property at Flinders Island, Bass Strait, to enlist in the AIF at Melbourne on 21 May 1915. His two years' previous service in the Victorian Rifles contributed to his appointment to second lieutenant, which occurred on 24 December

1915. Upon his arrival in France he was posted to the 8th Battalion, and was wounded on 30 September 1916. He did not return to his battalion until 15 January 1917. The wound was received during a successful night raid on enemy trenches for which Joynt was commended in divisional orders. On 31 December 1916 he was promoted to lieutenant.

Joynt won his Victoria Cross during the second phase of the final offensive that began with the battle of Amiens on 8 August. On 23 August, the 1st Australian and 32nd British Divisions attacked towards Herleville Wood. The 6th Battalion was on the right of the Australian line with the 8th Battalion 500 metres behind in reserve. Joynt went forward and found a company of the 6th Battalion that was disorganized after losing its officers. He reformed the men and urged them forward but they were again halted by intense fire from Plateau Wood. Joynt, who was then joined by a platoon from his own battalion, decided to seize Plateau Wood. A German post and fifty prisoners were quickly taken. Joynt then led his men along a trench across the plateau, capturing prisoners as they went, to within fifty metres of the machine-guns holding up the advance. At one stage twenty enemy advanced towards him with their rifles poised so Joynt covered their leader with a revolver and they surrendered. Finding another trench, Joynt was able to lead his men without casualties into the German position and so force them out of the wood. He returned to his battalion to find that his company com-

mander had been hit and that he was to assume command. From then until he was wounded in another attack three days later, he was always in the fight as the advance continued.

The war ended before Joynt rejoined his battalion and his AIF appointment finished on 11 June 1920; he had been promoted to captain on 29 October 1918. King George V decorated him with the Victoria Cross at Buckingham Palace on 12 July 1919.

For several of the early post war years Joynt farmed forty hectares at Berwick, Victoria, under the soldier settler scheme, but successive droughts forced him to move to Melbourne where he founded W.D. Joynt, printers and publishers. He was closely involved in the founding of the Legacy movement during this period and subsequently served on several of its committees.

From 1926 until 1933 he was an officer of the 6th Battalion, the Royal Melbourne Regiment, and in February 1930 was promoted to major and appointed second-in-command of the 6th. He returned to full-time duty when the 1939–45 war broke out and formed and commanded the 3rd Garrison Battalion. In 1941 he was commandant of Puckapunyal and from 1942 to 1944 was in charge of a similar large training camp at nearby Seymour. He was placed on the retired list on 10 October 1944.

Prior to retirement he was director of several publishing firms, president of the Old Melbournians, and an active head of his own firm. He broadcast to Australia from the dinner given by the lord mayor of

London at the Victoria Cross centenary celebrations in 1956. In 1975 he published *Saving the Channel Ports*, which was an account of his service in France in 1918, and followed this in 1979 with *Breaking the Road for the Rest*, which covered the remainder of his war service as well as peacetime. In 1983 he returned to Puckapunyal to witness the opening of the Donovan Joynt Victoria Cross Memorial Sportsmen's Club.

He married Edith A. Garrett on 19 March 1932 and lives at Windsor, Melbourne.

KENNY Thomas James Bede

RANK	Private
UNIT	2nd Battalion, 1st Brigade, 1st Division
DATE	9 April 1917
PLACE	Hermies, France

BEDE KENNY was born on 29 September 1896 at Paddington, New South Wales, eldest son of Austin James and Mary Christina Kenny. He was educated at Christian Brothers' College, Waverley, and began training as a chemist's assistant at Bondi. War interrupted this training and Kenny enlisted in the AIF on 23 August 1915 and embarked with the 13th reinforcements to the 2nd Battalion on 20 December. On arriving in Egypt he spent a brief period with the 54th Battalion prior to joining the 2nd on 27 February 1916. The 2nd went to France in March and Kenny fought in the battalion bombing platoon during the battle of Pozières four months later.

In March and April 1917, as British and Australian forces captured 'outpost villages' defended by Germans withdrawing to the newly constructed Hindenburg line, Kenny won the Victoria Cross. In the attack on the village of Hermies by the 2nd and 3rd Battalions on 9 April, Kenny's platoon came under heavy fire from a machine-gun post, which caused severe casualties. Kenny, under very heavy close-range fire, single-handedly rushed the enemy post and killed one man in front of the strong point who attempted to bar his way. He threw three bombs, the third of which knocked out the post. Kenny took the surviving occupants prisoner and a short while later the party following found him in occupation. A line of posts was then established around the eastern side of the village by Kenny's company and Hermies was completely sealed off.

Kenny was immediately appointed to lance corporal and soon after was evacuated to Britain with trench foot. He received his award at Buckingham Palace from King George V on 21 July 1917. He rejoined his unit at Hazebrouck in April 1918. On 26 June 1918 he was wounded during fighting in the Merris sector and was invalided to Australia on 24 August; he had been promoted to corporal on 1 August. Kenny received a tumultuous welcome when he arrived in Sydney on 9 October, and he was discharged on 12 December.

After the war Kenny first worked for Clifford Love & Company, manufacturers, importers and merchants, as northern New South Wales traveller, before joining the *Sunday Times* newspaper in Sydney. He later became a traveller for Penfolds Wines, trading with hotels from Surry Hills to Woolloomooloo. Kenny married Kathleen Dorothy Buckley at St Mary's Cathedral, Sydney, on 29 September 1927 (his birthday), and they had three children. His eldest daughter died in 1943 and his son in 1948, both from rheumatic fever. Kenny died from a combination of illnesses at Concord Repatriation Hospital, Sydney, on 15 April 1953. He was buried in the Roman Catholic section, Botany cemetery, Matraville. His name is commemorated in the Australian War Graves Garden of Remembrance, Rookwood. His widow attended the Victoria Cross centenary celebrations in London in 1956 and early in 1957 the Bede Kenny Memorial Ward was opened at Wentworth Private Hospital, Randwick, to provide beds for ex-servicemen ineligible for repatriation hospital treatment.

KEYSOR Leonard Maurice

RANK   Lance Corporal
UNIT   1st Battalion, 1st Brigade, 1st Division
DATE   7–8 August 1915
PLACE   Lone Pine trenches, Gallipoli Peninsula, Turkey

LEONARD KEYSOR was born on 3 November 1895 at Maida Vale, London, son of Benjamin Keysor. The name was sometimes spelt Keyzor. Educated at Tonnleigh Castle, Ramsgate, he moved to Canada to settle after his schooling. Three months before the outbreak of war he travelled to Australia and found employment in Sydney as a clerk.

Keysor enlisted in the AIF on 18 August 1914 and was posted to the 1st Battalion, which was just then forming at Randwick. Keysor embarked with his unit on 18 October, trained in the Middle East and participated in the Gallipoli landing on 25 April 1915; he was appointed lance corporal on 20 June. It was at Lone Pine that Keysor won the first of seven Victoria Crosses awarded to Australians for that battle. The Lone Pine operation commenced just before sunset on 6 August 1915 and before darkness fell the 1st Brigade had established a line of defensive posts around Lone Pine. Soon after dark the Turks moved in reinforcements and made the first of a series of bombing attacks that were to continue for three days. On 7 August Keysor was in a trench which was being heavily bombed by the enemy. At great risk to himself he picked up two live Turkish bombs and threw them back at the enemy. Although wounded, he kept throwing bombs. The next day, at the same place, he bombed the enemy out of a position which made his trench vulnerable. He was again wounded. Although he was marked for hospital he stayed in the trenches and threw bombs for another company which had lost its bomb throwers. Keysor kept throwing both Turkish bombs and crude Australian bombs, manufactured on the beach, for fifty hours before he allowed himself to be evacuated for treatment. On 9 August the enemy finally abandoned their counter-attack.

After Lone Pine Keysor went to Britain suffering from enteric fever. He was decorated by King George V at Buckingham Palace on 15 January 1916. Keysor rejoined his battalion in France in March 1916 and participated in the fighting at Pozières.

In December 1916 he was promoted to sergeant and on 13 January

1917 he was appointed second lieutenant; he was promoted to lieutenant on 28 July. On 17 November 1916 he had transferred to the 42nd Battalion and had been twice wounded while serving with that unit, on 28 March 1918 in the Méricourt-Sailly-le-Sec line and in a gas bombardment near Villers-Bretonneux on 26 May. Discharged on medical grounds on 12 December, Keysor returned to his pre-war employment as a clerk but, in 1920, returned to London and there, on 21 July 1921, married Gladys Benjamin at the Hill Street synagogue. There was one daughter of the marriage. Because he was living in Britain, he was the only Australian Victoria Cross winner of the 1914–18 war to attend the first two reunions of Victoria Cross winners, held in 1920 and 1929.

Keysor was, ironically, injured in 1927 while attempting to re-enact his bombing feats for a film entitled *For Valour*. He again lived at Maida Vale, entered an importing business, and was on the list of reserve officers of the Australian Military Forces but was rejected for service in 1939 on medical grounds. Keysor died in London of cancer on 12 October 1951 and was cremated after a memorial service at the Liberal Jewish Synagogue, St Johns Wood.

In 1977 Keysor's Victoria Cross and other service medals (except his 1914–15 Star) were purchased at auction in London by the Returned Services League. They are now displayed in the Hall of Valour at the Australian War Memorial.

LEAK John

RANK   Private
UNIT   9th Battalion, 3rd Brigade, 1st Division
DATE   23 July 1916
PLACE   Pozières, France

JOHN LEAK was born at Portsmouth, UK, in 1892, son of James Leak, a miner. He migrated to Australia as a young man and worked as a teamster in Queensland before enlisting in the AIF at Rockhampton on 28 January 1915; allotted to the 9th Battalion, he joined the unit on Gallipoli on 22 June. Leak went to France with the 9th and won the first of five Victoria Crosses awarded for the July–August 1916 fighting around Pozières.

The battle of the Somme opened disastrously on 1 July 1916 when thirteen British and five French divisions attacked, suffering heavy losses for little gain of territory. Pozières was to be captured on the first day of the battle but subsequent attacks brought the line to Pozières trench, which thwarted three planned British attacks. The 1st Australian Division was brought up to make the next attempt. A preliminary attack was made on 22 July but this was also unsuccessful. At 12.30 a.m. the next day, preceded by one of the most famous barrages of the war, the 1st Division overran Pozières trench and entered the town, having taken all objectives.

The 9th Battalion had attacked on the extreme right of the line and ran into the only heavy resistance where Pozières trench intersected a double trench system known as OG1 and OG2. A little further on was a bombing position which, with two machine-guns, held up the advance there. A bomb fight ensued in which the enemy 'egg' bombs out-ranged those of the Australians. Leak jumped out of his trench, ran forward under heavy machine-gun fire, and threw three bombs into the enemy post. He jumped into the post and bayoneted three unwounded bombers. Later, when the enemy drove the party back, Leak was the last to withdraw at each stage, and he kept bombing. When reinforcements arrived the whole trench was recaptured, although the fight for Pozières was to rage until the 27th, when the village was taken.

In mid-August the 1st Division came back into the line and made another assault, this time in the Mouquet farm area, 1500 metres north of Pozières. On the 21st Leak was wounded but rejoined his unit and fought with it until he was severely gassed at Hollebeke, Belgium, on 7 March 1918.

Leak married Beatrice Mary Chapman at Cardiff, Wales, on 30 December 1918. They then returned to Australia on 9 February 1919. He was discharged on 31 May in Queensland. For the next few years Leak shifted from Queensland to New South Wales, then to South Australia and finally on to Esperance, Western Australia, where he became a garage proprietor and mechanic. On 12 January 1927 he married Ada Victoria Bood-Smith and they had a family of four sons and three daughters.

In 1966 John Leak's Victoria Cross was the subject of controversy when it was revealed that a Victoria Cross purporting to be his was in the possession of a secondhand dealer. The real medal was still with Leak and the dealer was fined $40 on a charge of being in possession of a forged Victoria Cross without permission. Leak retired to Crafers, South Australia, and died of cardiac failure at Redwood Park on 20 October 1972. He was buried at Stirling cemetery in the Adelaide hills.

LOWERSON Albert David

RANK	Sergeant
UNIT	21st Battalion, 6th Brigade, 2nd Division
DATE	1 September 1918
PLACE	Mont St Quentin, north of Péronne, France

'ALBY' LOWERSON was born at Myrtleford, Victoria, on 2 August 1896, son of Henry and Mary Jane Lowerson. His childhood was spent in the Myrtleford district and he assisted his father in farming before taking up gold prospecting. He enlisted on 16 July 1915, was allotted to the 5th reinforcements to the 21st Battalion, embarked on 27 September, and joined his unit on 7 January 1916.

The unit arrived in France in late March, moving into a quiet sector of the line near Armentières. The battalion entered the battle of the Somme and saw the heavy fighting for Pozières Heights from 25 July until 7 August. After a fortnight's rest the battalion re-entered the line and Lowerson was wounded near Mouquet farm on 24 August. He was recommended for a Military Medal for his work at Armentières and Pozières but this was not granted. He was promoted to temporary corporal and confirmed in the rank on 1 November 1916. During second Bullecourt on 3 May 1917, he was again wounded and did not return to his unit until 26 October; he was confirmed as sergeant on 1 November 1916.

Lowerson's Victoria Cross was awarded for his courage and tactical skill during the attack on Mont St Quentin. He was also commended for his work in the week preceding that battle. At Virgin Wood, on 27 August, he had forced an enemy machine-gun crew, which had his platoon pinned down, to retire after he bombed it successfully. The following day, at Herbécourt, when the platoon was attacked on three sides, he mounted the parapet under heavy fire and bombed the enemy until the platoon reorganized.

On the morning of 31 August 1918, the 5th Brigade, 2nd Australian Division, seized the town of Mont St Quentin, which overlooked Péronne. German counter-attacks forced them out of the village but the 5th Brigade held on to the slopes. The 6th Brigade moved up to support the 5th Brigade the next morning. They were then to resume the attack, but strong opposition was encountered and the attackers were pinned down. After a heavy artillery barrage on the village the attack resumed at 1 p.m. and by 4 p.m. the Australians had virtually secured the objective and consolidation was well under way.

Lowerson was with the company which advanced on the right of the village, where it encountered extremely heavy fire. Several small strong points were taken out, but the troops on the left of the advance were pinned down by a heavily manned post which contained twelve machine-guns. Lowerson then organized a storming party of seven men and led a charge against the strong point which succeeded in capturing twelve machine-guns and thirty men. Although he was wounded in the right thigh, Lowerson organized the consolidation of the post and disposal of prisoners. Two days later he was evacuated for hospital treatment and returned to duty on 17 September. He fought on with his unit until wounded for a fourth time, on 5 October, at Montbrehain in the last action fought by Australian infantry in the 1914–18 war. He embarked from Britain on 1 April 1919, disembarking in Melbourne on 16 May where he was discharged medically unfit on 8 July 1919.

Lowerson returned to Myrtleford and began tobacco growing and dairy farming on a property at Merriang Estate named St Quentin. On 1 February 1929 he married Edith Larkin and they had one daughter.

Lowerson served in a training capacity during the 1939–45 war and after discharge returned to Myrtleford where he died of leukaemia on 15 December 1945. He was buried in the Myrtleford cemetery and a memorial headstone was erected over his grave in September 1949. In 1956 his widow attended the Victoria Cross centenary in London.

McCARTHY Lawrence (Laurence) Dominic

RANK   Lieutenant
UNIT   16th Battalion, 4th Brigade, 4th Division
DATE   23 August 1918
PLACE Near Madame Wood, west of Vermando-villers, France

L.D. McCARTHY was born at York, Western Australia, on 21 January 1892, the son of F. McCarthy. After schooling he was apprenticed for four years as a farmer to John White of Jennacubbine, via Northam. He also served in the 18th Light Horse for two and a half years before he moved to Lion Mill (now Mount

Helena), Perth, to work as a contractor. He enlisted on 16 October 1914 and at Blackboy Hill Camp he joined the newly formed 16th Battalion, embarking with that unit on 22 December.

At Gallipoli, on 13 May 1915, he was appointed lance corporal, and on 19 July was promoted to corporal. He was promoted to sergeant on 1 September and soon after was evacuated because of illness (probably dysentery) and did not rejoin the 16th until late November.

In France, on 8 March 1917, he was appointed company sergeant major, and on 2 April, during the first attack on Bullecourt, McCarthy was wounded. He was sent to Britain where he remained in hospitals and convalescent depots until 9 July when he rejoined his unit. He had been appointed second lieutenant on 10 April and on 1 November was promoted to lieutenant. McCarthy was posted for duty with the 13th Training Battalion at Tidworth, UK, on 31 January 1918, and did not rejoin the 16th until 8 August, the day on which the great Allied offensive commenced.

During the second phase of this offensive, on 23 August, McCarthy performed the deed for which he received the Victoria Cross. The 4th Division attacked towards Vermandovillers on 23 August in support of the 1st Australian and 32nd British Divisions, which were making the main effort that day. The 16th Battalion was next to the British division and quickly took its objective. However the British were held up by heavy machine-gun fire which threatened the 16th's flank. McCarthy decided to attack the nearest post, which he and Sergeant F.J. Robbins, DCM, MM, succeeded in reaching after a dash across fire-racked, open ground. They captured the machine-gun and continued to fight down the trench, inflicting heavy casualties and capturing three more machine-guns, until contact was made with the 16th Lancashire Fusiliers. McCarthy, during his advance, had killed twenty enemy and captured five machine-guns and fifty prisoners. When he jumped into the last trench the surrendering Germans closed in on him from all sides, took his revolver, patted him on the back and then allowed him to lead them back to Australian lines. He handed over 500 metres of captured trench to the British. This feat was described in the official history as being, next to Jacka's at Pozières, perhaps the most effective individual feat in the history of the AIF.

On 21 November McCarthy became ill again and was evacuated to hospital, where he learnt of the Victoria Cross award in December. He rejoined his unit on 7 January 1919, received the Victoria Cross from King George V at Buckingham Palace on 12 July, then returned to Australia on 20 December, where his appointment ceased on 6 August 1920.

He lived in Western Australia until 1926 when he moved to Victoria where, until 1934, he worked for the H.V. McKay Sunshine Harvester Company. McCarthy was then employed by Trustees, Executors and Agency Co. Ltd, Melbourne, until retirement. In 1956 he attended the Victoria Cross centenary in London and in 1965 visited Gallipoli for the fiftieth centenary of the landing.

McCarthy married Florence Minnie Norville in London on 25 January 1919 and their only child, Lawrence Norville McCarthy, was killed in action on Bougainville on 20 May 1945. L.D. McCarthy died at Heidelberg Repatriation Hospital on 25 May 1975 and after cremation his ashes were interred at Springvale cemetery.

His portrait by Charles Wheeler, DCM, and his medals (which include a *Croix de guerre* awarded by the French government) are displayed in the Australian War Memorial's Hall of Valour.

McDOUGALL Stanley Robert

RANK	Sergeant
UNIT	47th Battalion, 12th Brigade, 4th Division
DATE	28 March 1918
PLACE	Dernancourt, France

STANLEY MCDOUGALL was born at Recherche, Tasmania, on 23 July 1889, son of John Henry and Susannah McDougall. After schooling he took up blacksmithing and served his time at this trade. He was an excellent horseman, an expert marksman and a competent bushman; he also took up amateur boxing.

Illness prevented him from enlisting in the AIF until 31 August 1915 when he was accepted and posted to the 12th reinforcements to the 15th Battalion. His experience as a farrier was wanted by a light horse unit but McDougall chose to stay with the infantry. In Egypt, on 3 March 1916, he was taken on the strength of the 47th Battalion, a unit of the recently formed 12th Brigade. He trained with the 47th and embarked with them for France in June 1916.

Appointed lance corporal on 5 May 1917 he was promoted to corporal in September; he became temporary sergeant in November and this rank was confirmed on 23 January the following year.

When the great German offensive of 1918 commenced on 21 March the Australian Corps was ninety-six kilometres to the north, in Flanders. On 23 March, the 4th Australian Division received orders to move south. The 47th Battalion was one of the first two battalions to move into position on 27 March along the railway line between Dernancourt and Albert.

The night of 27–28 March was quiet until just on daybreak. McDougall was on watch at a post on the 47th's right flank when he heard approaching enemy. When a Lewis gun team was knocked out by an enemy bomb McDougall snatched up the Lewis gun and attacked two enemy machine-gun teams and killed their crews. He turned one of the captured machine-guns on to the enemy, killing several, and routing that wave.

Meanwhile, about fifty Germans had crossed the Australian-held railway. McDougall turned his gun on them before they had time to establish themselves behind the battalion. When his ammunition was spent he seized a bayonet and charged, killing three men and an enemy officer who was just about to kill an Australian officer. McDougall then used a Lewis gun on the enemy, killing many, and forcing the surrender of the remaining thirty-three enemy. For his actions McDougall was awarded the Victoria Cross.

Eight days after this action McDougall performed another deed in the same place and for this he was awarded the Military Medal. When another heavy enemy attack took place he managed to get a gun to an exposed position and enfilade the Germans at close quarters. Enemy fire hit the gun and damaged it, forcing McDougall to crawl about 300 metres under fire to obtain a replacement. When the Australians counter-attacked McDougall's platoon commander was killed, and McDougall commanded the platoon for the remainder of the action.

When the 47th Battalion was disbanded in May 1918 McDougall transferred to the 48th Battalion on 28 May 1918. At Windsor Castle on 19 August he was invested with the Victoria Cross by King George V, and shortly afterwards returned to Australia where he was discharged from the AIF in Tasmania on 15 December.

McDougall entered the Tasmanian Forestry Commission and in the early 1930s became an inspector in charge of all forests in the north-western part of Tasmania. On several occasions he performed outstanding organizational and rescue work during bushfires, especially those around Fitzgerald in 1934. Once his vehicle was burned from under him while he was attempting to shift a family's belongings from the path of a fire.

He was living at Scottsdale, Tasmania, when he visited London for the Victoria Cross centenary in 1956. The uniform he wore and the Lewis gun he used at Dernancourt are displayed in the Australian War Memorial's Hall of Valour along with his Victoria Cross. The Memorial holds a portrait of him by Frank Crozier.

McDougall died on 7 July 1968 at the North East Soldiers' Memorial Hospital, Scottsdale; he was survived by his wife Martha, née Anderson-Harrison, whom he had married in 1926; they did not have any children. His ashes were interred at Norwood cemetery, Mitchell, in the Australian Capital Territory.

McGEE Lewis

RANK   Sergeant
UNIT   40th Battalion, 10th Brigade, 3rd Division
DATE   4 October 1917
PLACE   East of Ypres, Belgium

LEWIS MCGEE was born in Campbell Town, Tasmania, on 13 May 1888, to John and Mary McGee. At the time he enlisted, on 1 March 1916, he was working as an engine driver for the Tasmanian Department of Railways and was living at Avoca with his wife, Eileen Rose, and their daughter. He was allotted to the 40th Battalion and joined it on 1 May. After training at Claremont, near Hobart, and Salisbury Plain, UK, the 40th went to France late in November. McGee was appointed lance corporal on 23 May 1916, promoted to corporal at Armentières on 4 December, and sergeant on 12 January 1917. He participated in the battle of Messines.

It was during the third of the step-by-step battles of the third battle of Ypres, the attack on Broodseinde Ridge, that McGee performed the acts for which he was awarded the Victoria Cross. As the Australians approached Broodseinde Ridge they encountered withering fire from trenches and thickly garrisoned pillboxes. Ten machine-guns were firing into the 40th from the front and left and the situation was critical. The left-hand company of the 40th was moved around through some half-sheltered ground in the New Zealand sector and was able to bring fire to bear on the Germans. A series of attacks on the pillboxes then commenced.

McGee's platoon was suffering severely and his company's advance was halted by machine-gun fire from a pillbox. McGee rushed the post armed only with a revolver, shooting some of the crew and capturing the rest, and enabling the advance to proceed. He reorganized the remnants of his platoon and led them through the rest of the advance. There were several more pillbox fights before the objective was completely taken. Nearly all pillboxes were overcome by acts of individual daring. By 9.12 a.m. the 40th was in occupation of its complete objective.

Although the battle of Broodseinde was a stunning victory, when it began to rain that afternoon any chance of exploiting the success vanished. The British attacked in what was known as the first battle of Passchendaele but were unsuccessful. Another attempt was made on 12 October, the second battle of Passchendaele, during which McGee was killed in action. He was buried at Tyne Cot cemetery, near Passchendaele.

In 1929 his wife remarried but remained in Avoca. McGee's Victoria Cross was sold at auction in 1984 and is in the possession of the Queen Victoria Museum of Art, Launceston, Tasmania.

McNAMARA Frank Hubert

RANK	Lieutenant
UNIT	No. 1 Squadron, Australian Flying Corps, AIF
DATE	20 March 1917
PLACE	Raid on Tel el Hesi, Palestine (now Israel)

FRANK MCNAMARA was born at Waranga, Rushworth, Victoria, on 4 April 1894, the son of W.F. McNamara. He was educated at Rushworth and Shepparton, and in 1913–14 studied at teachers' training college and the University of Melbourne. He then taught at Shepparton and Princes Hill, Melbourne, and later was head of Red Bluff, Mordialloc South and North Kooweerup schools.

McNamara joined the Senior Cadets in 1911 and the following year transferred to the Brighton Rifles (46th Infantry Battalion). In July 1913 he was appointed to a commission as second lieutenant and in 1914, at the outbreak of war, performed duty at the Queenscliff and Point Nepean fixed defences. In December 1914 he attended the fourth course at the Officers' Training School, Broadmeadows, and from February to May 1915 attended the third course at the Point Cook Flying School. He was posted as adjutant of No. 1 Squadron, Australian Flying Corps, when it was formed in January 1916.

From May to July 1916 he was in Britain for advanced training, attached to No. 42 Squadron, RFC. On his return to Egypt he was attached to No. 22 Squadron, RFC, as a flying instructor before he rejoined No. 1 Squadron with whom he flew his first operational sortie on 22 December.

During preparations for the allied attacks on Gaza in March 1917 McNamara performed the daring rescue which resulted in his being awarded the Victoria Cross. The incident occurred on 20 March after a raid on Tel el Hesi, which was on the main railway supply line between Junction Station and Tel el Sheria (now in Israel). The plane of an Aus-

tralian, Captain D.W. Rutherford, was hit by ground fire and forced to land behind enemy lines. McNamara, wounded in the thigh during the same attack, spotted enemy cavalry galloping towards Rutherford's plane. McNamara descended and Rutherford climbed on to McNamara's plane. An attempt to get airborne failed because McNamara's wounds prevented him from controlling the aircraft properly; the plane turned over in a gully. The two officers set fire to the machine and headed for Rutherford's plane, which they succeeded in starting. McNamara, weak from loss of blood, took off just as the hostile cavalry burst into the clearing. He flew the machine 115 kilometres back to his aerodrome.

McNamara was promoted to captain and flight commander on 10 April 1917 but in September was invalided to Australia where his appointment ended on 31 January 1918. The following September he was reappointed to the AFC with his former seniority and rank. He became an aviation instructor with the permanent forces, and later with the Australian Air Corps. He received the Victoria Cross from Edward, Prince of Wales, on 27 May 1920 at Government House, Melbourne, during the prince's tour of Australia.

When the RAAF was inaugurated in 1921 McNamara transferred to it as a flight lieutenant and until July 1922 served as a staff officer (operations and intelligence) at RAAF Headquarters, Melbourne. He became Officer Commanding, 1 Flying Training School (1 FTS), Point Cook, from March 1924 with the rank of squadron leader. At this time he married Helene Marcelle Bluntschli. In June 1925 he went to Britain on exchange duty with the RAF and he returned in November 1927 to become second-in-command, 1 FTS; in October 1930 he became its commanding officer. A year later he was promoted to wing commander and in February 1933 was posted to No. 1 Aircraft Depot and RAAF Station, Laverton, as commanding officer. In 1928 he returned to Melbourne University part time and on 23 December 1933 he was awarded the degree of Bachelor of Arts. In 1936 he was promoted to group captain and the following year attended the Imperial Defence College. His next posting was as air liaison officer at the Air Ministry, London. When the 1939–45 war broke out he was promoted to air commodore and in 1942 to air vice marshal, and was appointed Air Officer Commanding RAAF Headquarters, London. From late 1942 until the end of the war he was on loan to the RAF as Air Officer Commanding British Forces, Aden. He returned to London to become RAAF representative at the Ministry of Defence and in July 1946 was appointed Director of Education at the headquarters of the British Occupation Administration, Westphalia, Germany.

After retiring from the service he was a member of the National Coal Board from 1947 until 1959. He lived at Gerrards Cross, Buckinghamshire, UK, until his death on 2 November 1961. His funeral at St Joseph's Priory, Austin Wood, Gerrards Cross, was attended by many mourners. He was survived by his wife, a son and a daughter.

In addition to the Victoria Cross McNamara was awarded the CBE in the New Year's honours list of 1938 and in 1945 was made a Companion of the Order of the Bath. A large painting by H. Septimus Power, which depicts McNamara's daring rescue, hangs in the Australian War Memorial.

MACTIER Robert

RANK	Private
UNIT	23rd Battalion, 6th Brigade, 2nd Division
DATE	1 September 1918
PLACE	Mont St Quentin, north of Péronne, France

ROBERT MACTIER was born at Tatura, Victoria, on 17 May 1890, to Robert and Christina Mactier. He was educated at the Tatura state school and afterwards worked on his father's property, Reitcam ('Mactier' reversed).

Mactier enlisted at Seymour on 1 March 1917, was posted to the 19th reinforcements to the 23rd Battalion, and left Australia on 11 May. He disembarked in Britain on 20 July and trained before joining the 23rd in France on 23 November.

Mactier's gallant action, for which he was awarded the Victoria Cross, occurred during the 23rd's attempt to move into position. On 31 August,

the 6th Brigade had occupied Florina trench and expected to attack Péronne next morning. However, they were ordered to hand the position over to the 14th Brigade and move sideways across the main Péronne road into Gottlieb trench, where they would commence to attack at 6 a.m. They would pass through the 5th Brigade on the slopes below Mont St Quentin and take the village which overlooked Péronne. Bombing patrols were sent forward to overcome several strong points between Florina and Gottlieb trenches, but as they did not clear the enemy, the battalion was unable to move. At this stage Mactier, who had been sent forward as a runner to investigate, ran forward to the barricade. He threw a bomb, climbed over the wire, closed with and killed the machine-gun garrison of eight men with revolver and bombs, and threw the enemy gun over the parapet. He rushed forward another twenty metres and jumped into the middle of another garrison of six men who surrendered immediately. He charged a third post, bombing and killing the garrison. He was attacking a fourth enemy position when a machine-gun swung round and killed him instantly. His solo effort, however, enabled the companies of the 23rd to move to their 'jumping-off' trench as the barrage fell on Mont St Quentin.

Mactier was buried in the Hem farm cemetery, Hem-Monacu. His two sisters represented him at the Victoria Cross centenary in London in 1956. His name is commemorated in a soldiers' club at Watsonia Barracks, Melbourne, which was opened by the Minister for the Army in May 1960. His Victoria Cross was presented by his family to the Australian War Memorial in 1983 and is now displayed in the Hall of Valour. He never married.

MAXWELL Joseph

RANK	Lieutenant
UNIT	18th Battalion, 5th Brigade, 2nd Division
DATE	3 October 1918
PLACE	Beaurevoir line, near Estrées, France

'JOE' MAXWELL was born at Forest Lodge, Sydney, on 10 February 1896 to John and Elizabeth Maxwell. He worked as a boilermaker's apprentice at an engineering works near Newcastle prior to his enlistment in the AIF. Maxwell had served previously for three years in the Senior Cadets and for two years in the militia. On 6 February 1915 he

was posted to the 18th Battalion and he was taken on strength of that unit on 24 June. In August he went with his unit to Gallipoli. After the evacuation from Gallipoli in December he was in Egypt until his unit went to France in late March 1916. On 7 August 1917 he had become a company sergeant major and by October a sergeant.

Maxwell's first decoration, the Distinguished Conduct Medal, was won on 20 September, in an attack near Westhoek, during the third battle of Ypres. Maxwell took command of a platoon, whose officer had been killed, and led it in the attack. Later, when he noticed one of the newly captured positions under heavy fire, he dashed to it and led the men to a safer and more tactically secure position, thus saving many lives. On 29 September he was appointed second lieutenant and on 1 January 1918 was promoted to lieutenant.

In early March 1918 Maxwell won his second decoration, the Military Cross. He was in charge of a scouting patrol near Ploegsteert and, having obtained the required information, ordered the patrol to withdraw. He, and three others, were covering the withdrawal of the main body to their lines when he noticed a party of approximately thirty Germans. He recalled the patrol and attacked the enemy with rifles and bombs; the Germans quickly withdrew leaving three dead and one wounded.

On 9 August, the second day of the battle of Amiens, the 18th was preparing to attack near Rainecourt. In the initial moments all officers in the company, except Maxwell, became casualties. Under his leadership the company attacked on time, still under heavy fire. A tank which preceded the Australian advance was knocked out by an enemy 77 mm gun. Maxwell, very close to it, rushed over and opened the hatch, freeing its occupants just before it burst into flames. After escorting the tank commander to comparative safety Maxwell went forward, led the company in the attack, and succeeded in reaching and consolidating the objective. For this he earned a bar to his Military Cross.

His major decoration, the Victoria Cross, was gained in the breaching of the Hindenburg line around Beaurevoir and Montbrehain in early October, at the end of Australian involvement in the fighting in the 1914–18 war.

Early in the advance, on 3 October, Maxwell's company commander was severely wounded. Maxwell immediately took charge. When the company reached the enemy wire they found it extremely effective and well covered by machine-gun fire. Maxwell, single-handedly, found a way through the wire, captured the most dangerous gun, killed three enemy and took another four prisoner. This enabled his company to move through the wire and take the objective. Later he again single-handedly silenced a gun which was holding up a flank company.

When Maxwell learnt from an English-speaking prisoner that some Germans in a nearby post wished to surrender he took two men to the position. About twenty Germans surrounded them and seized their weapons. At that moment a five-minute barrage came down and Maxwell took advantage of the confusion, pulled out a concealed revolver and shot two of the enemy and then escaped with the other two of his party. He received the Victoria Cross from King George V at Buckingham Palace on 8 March 1919.

Maxwell returned to Australia in May 1919 and after demobilization on 8 August worked as a gardener in Canberra, Moree, and the Maitland district. He married twice. The first marriage to Mabel Maxwell at Woollahra on 14 February 1921 ended in divorce in 1926. On 6 March 1956 he married Anne Martin at the Registrar-General's Office. In collaboration with Hugh Buggy he published, in 1932, *Hell's Bells* and *Mademoiselles*. He made several attempts to enlist for service at the start of the 1939–45 war and eventually went to Queensland where, in June 1940, he enlisted under an alias. He was discovered and given a position in a training battalion.

Maxwell attended the Victoria Cross centenary in London in 1956. He lived in Matraville, New South Wales, for several years before his sudden death from a heart attack on 6 July 1967. After cremation, his ashes were interred at Eastern Suburbs Crematorium in Botany. He was survived by his wife Anne who donated his medals to the Army Museum at Victoria Barracks, Paddington, New South Wales. Four months after his death, on 27 October, a club for soldiers bearing Maxwell's name was opened at Holsworthy Barracks.

MOON Rupert Vance

RANK	Lieutenant
UNIT	58th Battalion, 15th Brigade, 5th Division
DATE	12 May 1917
PLACE	Near Bullecourt, France

'MICK' MOON was born at Bacchus Marsh, Victoria, on 14 August 1892, to Arthur and Helen Moon. His earliest years were spent at Maffra, in the Gippsland district, and he was educated at Kyneton Grammar School. After school he joined the National Bank and worked at Kyneton, Casterton, South Melbourne, Bairnsdale and Maffra.

Before the war he had served in the 13th Light Horse and 8th Infantry Regiments and upon enlistment, on 21 August 1914, joined the Light Horse and was posted to the 4th Light Horse Regiment. He served with the 4th on Gallipoli, was appointed lance corporal in November 1915 and became a sergeant early in March 1916. On 9 September he was commissioned second lieutenant and posted to the 58th Battalion; he was promoted to lieutenant on 6 April 1917.

On 12 May 1917 the 58th was supporting the British 7th Division in an attack near Bullecourt. The attack commenced on time and Moon's platoon was given the task of 'taking out' a concrete machine-gun shelter which lay between the opposing trenches. Moon, wounded early in the attack, successfully led his men in the capture of the shelter. He then rallied them for an attack on the enemy trench and, although wounded a second time, organized a Lewis gun team to bring effective fire to bear on the Germans, causing them to flee. He followed, but was forced back, so he organized for grenades to be thrown at the enemy who were sheltering in a cutting. With some other men he attacked the position and forced the Germans into dug-outs where they were effectively trapped. Moon was wounded for a third time (in the leg and foot) in the fight for this cutting.

As the reinforcements came through to mop up, Moon and two fellow officers decided to withdraw their men a short distance and consolidate to escape the persistent sniper fire. Just before the move was carried out, Moon, who was peering over the cutting to ascertain enemy locations, was shot in the jaw. He insisted, however, on seeing the new position occupied before he allowed two men to take him to the rear. For his conspicuous bravery he was awarded the Victoria Cross.

After recovering from his wounds Moon was invested with his Victoria Cross by King George V at Buckingham Palace on 3 August 1917, and in March 1918 he returned to Australia for two months. In May he returned to France and, on 5 February 1919, was promoted to temporary captain. He returned to Australia in June where his AIF appointment was terminated on 4 October. He transferred to the reserve of officers with the rank of honorary captain.

Moon had various jobs in the years between the wars. First he worked in Malaya as assistant manager of a rubber plantation. He then worked as a bookkeeper and jackaroo on a property near Corowa, New South Wales, before returning to the National Bank. After holding posts at various branches, including North Melbourne and Foster, he became an accountant with the Geelong firm of Dennys Lascelles. Later he was its managing director until he retired in 1960 although he remained a director until 1975.

On 18 December 1931 he married Susan Alison May Vincent and they had one son and one daughter. He served with the Volunteer Defence Corps during the 1939–45 war. On 9 September 1942 he was appointed captain in the 6th Victorian Battalion and posted as assistant staff captain of the South West Group from January 1943 until September 1944. He lived at Calder Park, Mount Duneed, and more recently at Barwon Heads, Victoria.

A portrait by W.B. McInnes hangs in the Australian War Memorial's Hall of Valour. The R.V. Moon Soldiers' Club at the 1st Battalion, Royal Victoria Regiment, depot at Sunshine was named in his honour.

At the time of writing he is the senior Victoria Cross winner, having won the award earlier than any other Victoria Cross winner living.

MURRAY Henry William

RANK   Captain
UNIT   13th Battalion, 4th Brigade, 4th Division
DATE   4–5 February 1917
PLACE Stormy trench, northeast of Gueudecourt, France

H.W. MURRAY was born on 30 December 1884, near Launceston, Tasmania, to E.K. and Clarissa Murray. He obtained his early military training in the Launceston Artillery before he moved to Western Australia. He was employed as a timbergetter in the south-west of the state when he enlisted in the AIF on 13 October 1914. He was posted as a machine-gunner in the 16th Battalion and he landed with that unit at Gallipoli on 25 April 1915. On 13 May he was appointed lance corporal and within a month of landing had won the Distinguished Conduct Medal and a mention in corps orders. He was particularly conspicuous on the day after the landing and during the attack on Hill 971 on 8 August.

When names were forwarded for possible commissions in the British 29th Division Murray's was included. The commanding officer of the 13th learnt of this and sought Murray as machine-gun officer of his battalion. Thus in the one day he rose from lance corporal to second lieutenant. Murray was twice wounded on Gallipoli, on 30 May and 8 August. On 20 January 1916 he was promoted to lieutenant and on 1 March to captain. He moved to France with his unit in late March and on 14–15 August 1916 won the Distinguished Service Order at Mouquet farm. On this occasion he actually reached the remains of the farm with his men but was met by a numerically superior enemy force and had to retire. He conducted the retirement so that his force of one hundred men was extricated safely and a number of prisoners were brought back as well. It finally took a force of 3000 to capture the farm.

In the late winter of 1916–17 orders were given for I Anzac Corps to adopt a more offensive attitude in order to keep the Germans under strain. The 15th Battalion seized Stormy trench (also called Cloudy trench) on the night of 1–2 February 1917 but were forced to withdraw because of inadequate artillery support. Three nights later the 13th Battalion was given the same objective. Murray, leading A Company, seized the right of Stormy trench after stiff resistance and then consolidated for the expected counter-attacks. The Germans counter-attacked three times. On the last attack Murray gathered together twenty bombers and organized a brilliant charge which drove off the enemy. Throughout the night his company suffered heavy casualties through concentrated shell-fire and on one occasion gave up a short section of ground. Murray rallied his command and saved the situation. He headed bombing parties, led bayonet charges and carried wounded to safety. By daylight on the 5th his party was solidly in occupation and the Germans did not attack again. For his conspicuous bravery Murray was awarded the Victoria Cross.

Two months later seven battalions of the 4th Australian Division, including the 13th Battalion, attacked the Hindenburg line near Bullecourt. Despite the failure of tanks to cut the wire, the Hindenburg line was breached. The troops in the newly won trenches were quickly isolated and although Murray was not the senior officer forward, many sought him out for direction as he was the best known leader in his brigade. Mislead by wrong reports, the artillery did not fire against the German counter-attacks and, with ammunition running low, the Australians were forced out of the Hindenburg line. The 4th Division lost 2339 out of about 3000 men engaged, including 1170 taken prisoner. For his actions Murray was awarded the bar to his Distinguished Service Order.

On the same day as this battle Murray was promoted to temporary major and the rank was confirmed on 12 July; at the end of the year he temporarily commanded the 13th. On 8 March 1918 he was promoted to lieutenant colonel and took command of the 4th Machine Gun Battalion a week later. In the last months of the war he earned the French *Croix de guerre* and, in September, he and other specialist officers were attached to the II American Corps for a month in an advisory role.

In May 1919 he was created a Companion of the Order of St Michael and St George. In addition to his many decorations Murray was mentioned in dispatches on four occasions. While awaiting repatriation, Murray and W.D. Joynt [q.v.] were given charge of parties of farmers in the AIF who elected, under the education schemes, to tour farming districts in Britain and Denmark to study agricultural methods. Murray learnt much of value and after his AIF appointment ended on 9 March 1920 he looked for a suitable sheep-farming property. He took up a property of 3230 hectares eighty kilometres from Richmond, northern Queensland. On 30 November 1927 he married Ellen P. Cameron; they had a son and a daughter.

Murray returned to the active list on 21 July 1939 to command the 26th Battalion (the Logan and Albert Regiment), and led this unit until 7 August 1942 when he joined his local battalion of the Volunteer Defence Corps. He commanded the 23rd Regiment of the Volunteer Defence Corps until 7 February 1944 when he retired from active military duty.

In 1956, accompanied by his wife, he attended the Victoria Cross centenary in London. After a motor accident on the Condamine Highway, Murray died of a heart attack in Miles hospital on the Darling Downs on 7 January 1966.

His portrait, by George Bell, hangs in the Hall of Valour, Australian War Memorial.

NEWLAND James Ernest

RANK	Captain
UNIT	12th Battalion, 3rd Brigade, 1st Division
DATE	8 April and 15 April 1917
PLACE	West of Boursies and Lagnicourt, France

JAMES NEWLAND was born at Highton, Geelong, Victoria, on 22 August 1881. He enlisted and served in South Africa with the 4th Battalion, Australian Commonwealth Horse. When he returned to Australia he joined the Victorian artillery, served with that corps for five years, and subsequently became a permanent member of the instructional staff of the Commonwealth Military Forces. He was stationed in Tasmania but transferred to the AIF on 22 August 1914 as regimental quartermaster sergeant of the 12th Battalion. He was wounded on Gallipoli shortly after the landing, but on 22 May 1915 was commissioned second

lieutenant; promotion to lieutenant came on 15 October. His battalion embarked for France late in March and Newland was adjutant with the rank of captain. In the 12th's first major battle, at Poziéres, he was mentioned in dispatches for conspicious courage, leadership and organization.

In December 1916 he left the 12th for duty with Headquarters, 2nd Brigade, but was posted to his former unit as A Company commander for the February 1917 drive on Bapaume. On 19 January 1917 he was recommended for the *Croix de guerre* but the recommendation was not forwarded. He was wounded on 26 February but returned to his unit for the April attacks by the 1st Australian Division on Boursies, Demicourt and Hermies, the last three villages before the Hindenburg line. It was decided to capture all three on 9 April, the day the main British spring offensive opened at Arras. In order to mislead the Germans on the direction from which Hermies would be assaulted, a preliminary operation to the north of Boursies was staged on 8 April as a feint.

In the initial advance on Boursies, which began at 3 a.m., Newland's company was confronted by heavy fire and many casualties were sustained. Newland then successfully led a bombing attack on a ruined mill located about 400 metres short of the village. The attack dislodged the enemy and enabled the company to move on the objective. The Australians then came under heavy shellfire during the day and at 10 p.m. the Germans launched a violent counter-attack. By his personal exertion, disregard of fire and judicious use of reserves, he succeeded in dispersing the counter-attack and holding the position. The 12th was relieved by the 11th on 10 April.

On the night of 14 April the unit came back into the line to relieve the 9th at Lagnicourt. An hour before dawn on 15 April Newland informed battalion headquarters that the enemy were attacking. The whole front of the 1st Australian Division was in fact being attacked. The Germans broke through the company to the right of A Company, which was being led by Newland, and forced them back. Newland consolidated his men on the very position which Captain Cherry [q.v.] had held during the taking of Lagnicourt three weeks earlier. By personal example he encouraged his men to repel the combined attack and although the enemy renewed the attack three or four times Newland's company held out. The 9th Battalion came to reinforce the 12th and the two units combined to counter-attack. The line was restored about 11 a.m. For his conspicuous bravery and devotion to duty Newland was awarded the Victoria Cross.

On 6 May Newland was wounded at the second battle of Bullecourt. He was invested with the Victoria Cross by King George V on 21 July at Buckingham Palace and embarked six days later for return to Australia where his AIF appointment was terminated on 2 March 1918. He continued to serve as an officer of the permanent forces and between the wars held various appointments, including adjutant and quartermaster to the 8th, 49th, 52nd, 38th and 12th Battalions, area officer and recruiting officer; he was promoted to major on 1 May 1930. After the outbreak of the 1939–45 war Newland was seconded for duty as quartermaster instructor at Headquarters 4th Division. On 10 May 1940 he took up his final appointment as quartermaster, A Branch, Army Headquarters, Melbourne, and in August 1941 was placed on the retired list with the honorary rank of lieutenant colonel.

In November 1935 Newland was awarded the Meritorious Service Medal. After he retired from the army he became Assistant Commissioner of the Australian Red Cross Society in the Northern Territory. He died suddenly at his home at Caulfield, Victoria, on 19 March 1949 and was survived by his wife, Vivienne Heather, and a daughter. He was buried in the Methodist section of Brighton cemetery. In 1984 his daughters donated his Victoria Cross and other service medals to the Australian War Memorial for display in the Hall of Valour.

O'MEARA Martin

RANK	Private
UNIT	16th Battalion, 4th Brigade, 4th Division
DATE	9–12 August 1916
PLACE	Poziéres, France

MARTIN O'MEARA was born at Lorrha, County Tipperary, Ireland, on 31 December 1885. He migrated to Australia as a young man and was working as a labourer and sleeper cutter at Bowling Pool, via Collie, Western Australia, prior to his enlistment in the AIF at Blackboy Hill Camp on 19 August 1915. He was allotted to the 12th reinforcements to the 16th Battalion and embarked at Fremantle on HMAT *Ajana* on 22 December. By 6 August the 2nd Australian Division had taken Poziéres Heights and was then relieved by the 4th Australian Division which was to continue the attack northwards towards Mouquet farm. Three days later the 16th Battalion moved up to occupy the forward trenches. At mid-night the unit began its assault against Point 78 and succeeded in capturing its objective against strong resistance. At 1 a.m. on the 11th the advance began again but at daylight the enemy commenced a heavy bombardment and kept up the shelling until noon. A counter-attack commenced from the direction of Mouquet farm at about 2.30 p.m. and fifteen minutes later the German line began to move in. When the Germans approached the 16th Battalion's front they were hit by a withering fire from the defenders and in a quarter of an hour the attack had broken up and the remaining enemy retreated. The 16th contacted corps headquarters by carrier pigeon and twenty minutes later heavy artillery batteries shelled Mouquet farm and the valley. That night the battalion carried out further exploratory advances; the battalion also sustained casualties in a return German bombardment.

During these four days of heavy fighting, O'Meara, a stretcher bearer, repeatedly went out and brought in wounded from no man's land despite intense artillery and machine-gun fire; he was busy during the whole series of operations, especially in the critical barrage and counter-attack period. Four times he carried water and supplies forward under bursting shells and then returned carrying wounded. On one occasion, he volunteered to carry ammunition and bombs to a portion of trench which was receiving heavy shelling.

He was wounded on three occasions; on 12 August 1916 just after performing the above-mentioned acts, and in April and August 1917. On 13 March 1918 he was promoted to corporal and on 30 August to sergeant.

O'Meara embarked for return to Australia on 15 September 1918 and was demobilized in Perth on 30 November 1919. His health broke down completely and he spent the rest of his life in a mental hospital at Claremont. He died on 20 December 1935 and was buried in the Roman Catholic section of Karrakatta cemetery, Perth, with full military honours.

O'Meara never married and had no relatives in Australia. His will, made in 1917 during a visit to Ireland, directed that monies raised in various parishes as a testimonial to him should be devoted to the restoration of the ancient abbey at Lorrha. His Victoria Cross passed into the custody of the 16th Battalion at Perth.

PEELER Walter

RANK	Lance Corporal
UNIT	3rd Pioneer Battalion, 3rd Division
DATE	4 October 1917
PLACE	Broodseinde, east of Ypres, Belgium

'WALLY' PEELER was born on 9 August 1887 at Castlemaine, Victoria. He worked on his parents' orchard at Barkers Creek and then in a Castlemaine foundry. In 1908 he married Emma Kathleen Hewitt. He enlisted on 17 February 1916 while working in the Leongatha district, and was posted to the machine-gun section of the 3rd Pioneer Battalion. Appointed lance corporal in France on 6 November 1916, he was twice wounded — on 7 June and 20 October 1917.

Peeler won his Victoria Cross on 4 October 1917 during the fight for Broodseinde Ridge, in the third of the step-by-step battles during the third battle of Ypres, the battle of

Broodseinde Ridge. Peeler was attached to the 37th Battalion to provide anti-aircraft fire with his Lewis gun during the attack, but he actually led the fight at several points in the advance.

When he encountered an enemy party sniping at the advancing troops from a shell-hole he rushed the position and accounted for nine of the enemy and cleared the way for the advance. He performed similar acts on two subsequent occasions and each time accounted for a number of the enemy. He was, at one stage, directed to a position from which an enemy machine-gun fired on the Australians. He located and killed the gunner. The rest of the enemy party ran to a close dug-out but were dislodged by a bomb and when they ran out they were shot by Peeler. In all he accounted for over thirty of the enemy. At 7.15 a.m. the objective was captured. This, the third and greatest stroke within a fortnight, had badly shaken the Germans. However, rain in the afternoon prevented the exploitation of this success and Passchendaele was not to fall until November when it was captured by the Canadians.

Peeler received his decoration from King George V at Buckingham Palace in January 1918. In May he was promoted to temporary corporal and on 30 July to sergeant. He returned to Australia in October 1918 and was discharged from the AIF on 10 December.

Peeler joined the Victorian Department of Lands, and for six years was a member of its soldier settler branch. He resigned and took up an orchard in his home district but abandoned this venture and returned to Melbourne where, with L.D. McCarthy [q.v.], he was employed by the H.V. McKay Harvester works at Sunshine. Upon the completion of Victoria's Shrine of Remembrance in Melbourne in 1934, he was appointed custodian, a position which he held until he retired in 1964. He was a member of the Corps of Commissioners for many years.

Peeler did, however, enlist for service in the 1939–45 war and became a member of 2/2nd Pioneer Battalion when it formed in May 1940. He served throughout the Syrian campaign (June–July 1941) as a company quartermaster sergeant with the rank of staff sergeant and at Merdjayoun, late in June, led a party out in front of the line at night looking for wounded, four of whom were recovered. Early in 1942 he went with the 2/2nd Pioneer Battalion to Java as part of Blackforce, commanded by Brigadier A.S. Blackburn [q.v.]. When Java surrendered to the Japanese Peeler became a prisoner and, despite his age, survived harsh treatment and returned to Australia in 1945.

In the Queen's birthday honours of 10 June 1961, he was awarded the British Empire Medal. He visited London in 1956 for the Victoria Cross centenary and in September 1959 attended the opening of a soldiers' club which bore his name at Casula, New South Wales.

Peeler died on 23 May 1968 at his home in Moore Street, South Caulfield, Victoria. His second wife Kathleen died a year later. Both are buried in the same grave in Brighton cemetery. His name is commemorated in the Victoria Garden of Remembrance at Springvale. His medals are now displayed in the Hall of Valour at the Australian War Memorial.

POPE Charles

RANK   Lieutenant
UNIT   11th Battalion, 3rd Brigade, 1st Division
DATE   15 April 1917
PLACE   Louverval, France

CHARLES POPE was born at Mile End, London, on 5 March 1883. He was educated at Navestock and later migrated to Canada where he was employed by Canadian Pacific Railways. He returned to London in 1906 and joined the Chelsea division of the Metropolitan Police Force, but resigned in 1910 and again migrated, this time to Perth, Australia, where he joined an insurance company.

Pope enlisted in the AIF on 25 August 1915 and was posted to the 11th Battalion. He was appointed second lieutenant on 10 February 1916 and promoted to lieutenant on 26 December.

The exploit for which Pope was awarded the Victoria Cross occurred during the Lagnicourt counter-attack. Parts of four German divisions attacked the lines held by the 1st Australian Division early on the morning of 15 April 1917. The 11th Battalion held an extended front of nearly four kilometres between Lagnicourt and Louverval. Pope commanded one of three posts well forward on a protruding spur in the centre of the Australian line. The post he and his men occupied was considered crucial and his orders were to hold it at all costs. Pope's post was quickly surrounded by a much larger German force. Pope sent a runner back to get more ammunition but the resupplying force were blocked by superior German forces. When all hope was gone Pope still ordered his men to hang on. He was killed in front of his post. The 10th Battalion reinforced the 11th and the gaps in the line were covered and held, but the 11th had suffered heavy casualties.

Pope had married in Australia and was survived by his widow Edith Mary, a son and a daughter. His permanent grave is in Moeuvres communal cemetery extension, France. His wife remarried in 1929. Pope's brother, John, was also killed in action in France.

RUTHVEN William

RANK	Sergeant
UNIT	22nd Battalion, 6th Brigade, 2nd Division
DATE	19 May 1918
PLACE	Ville-sur-Ancre, France.

'RUSTY' RUTHVEN was born at Collingwood, Victoria, on 21 May 1893 to P. and Catherine Ruthven. He was educated at Vere Street school, became a mechanical engineer and was occupied in the timber industry when he enlisted on 19 April 1915. Posted as a reinforcement to the 22nd Battalion, he was taken on the strength of that unit on 25 October on Gallipoli. The 22nd went to France late in March 1916 and at Fleurbaix, on 17 April, Ruthven was wounded. When he rejoined the battalion on 12 August he was appointed lance corporal. Ruthven was confirmed as corporal on 2 October and, on 13 December was promoted to temporary sergeant, a rank he retained until his appointment as second lieutenant on 1 July 1918. He was wounded a second time on 11 June near Méricourt.

Ruthven won his Victoria Cross during the comparatively quiet period between the saving of Amiens and the start of the final offensive in August. For four months the Australian Corps maintained offensive operations which consisted of raids and local enterprises known as peaceful penetration. The 6th Brigade, in a clever and spectacular attack, captured the high ground near Ville-sur-Ancre. The 22nd supplied most of the troops engaged.

During the advance on Ville-sur-Ancre, on 19 May 1918, Ruthven's company suffered many casualties and his company commander was severely wounded. Ruthven then assumed command of company headquarters and thus effectively led this part of the assault. As the leading wave approached its objective it encountered heavy machine-gun fire so Ruthven, without hesitation, bombed the post, rushed the position and bayoneted one of the crew and captured the gun. He then encountered some enemy coming out of a shelter. He wounded two of the enemy and took another six prisoners. He reorganized the men in his vicinity and established a post in the second objective. When he observed enemy movement in a sunken road nearby he went over armed only with a revolver. He shot two enemy who refused to come out of their dug-outs and then, single-handedly, mopped up the post, capturing thirty-two men. During the remainder of the day he moved up and down the position, ignoring the enemy fire, and supervised the consolidation and encouraged his men. At 2.30 a.m. (half an hour after the assault was launched), the battalion began to dig in on the crest of the slope overlooking Morlancourt. Ruthven was wounded on 11 June in front of Méricourt and on 1 July he was appointed second lieutenant. He received the ribbon of the Victoria Cross from General John Monash at a presentation ceremony held near Camon, France, on 13 July 1918. His Victoria Cross was presented by King George V at Buckingham Palace on 16 August 1918.

Later that month he embarked for Australia where on 19 October he was promoted to lieutenant. His AIF appointment was terminated on 11 December and he returned to engineering work in Melbourne. He continued to serve in the 22nd Battalion until 1 June 1922 when he transferred to the reserve of officers. In 1923, however, he left to take up a 323 hectare property at Werrimull in the Mallee as a soldier settler. He returned to Collingwood in 1931 and went into business as a master carrier. Not long afterwards he was elected to the Collingwood council and served for twelve years, including a term as mayor in 1945. He was a foundation member of the Collingwood Football Social Club and was official timekeeper of the Collingwood Football Club from 1940 until 1946.

In December 1941 he was appointed from the reserve of officers to the 3rd Australian Garrison Battalion, with which he served until January 1943. Ruthven then served with other garrison units until he ceased full-time duty on 30 August 1944. He was promoted to captain on 30 June 1943 and to major on 1 March 1944. In 1945 he was elected to the Victorian Legislative Assembly as member for Preston, and held the seat of Reservoir from 1955 until he retired in 1961.

He married Irene M. White on 20 December 1919 and their family consisted of one son and a daughter. He visited London in 1956 for the Victoria Cross centenary celebrations. Ruthven lived in West Preston, Melbourne, prior to his death at Heidelberg Repatriation Hospital on 12 January 1970. He was given a full military funeral at All Saints' Church, Preston. He was cremated and his ashes interred at Fawkner cemetery.

A soldiers' club at Broadmeadows army camp was named after him in 1959, and a new railway station in Reservoir was named after him in 1963. His medals, which were presented to the Australian War Memorial in 1973, and a portrait of him by George Bell, are included in the Australian War Memorial's Hall of Valour.

RYAN (Edward) John (Frances)

RANK Private
UNIT 55th Battalion, 14th Brigade, 5th Division
DATE 30 September 1918
PLACE Near Bellicourt, France

JOHN RYAN was born at Tumut, New South Wales, in February 1890, to Michael and Eugenie Ryan. He was employed as a labourer when he enlisted at Wagga Wagga on 1 December 1915. He enlisted as John Ryan and was always known as such. His full name was Edward John Frances Ryan. He participated in the 'Kangaroos' recruiting march which marched 500 kilometres from Wagga to Sydney. He embarked as a reinforcement to the 55th Battalion on 14 June 1916 and joined his unit in France on 23 September. He remained with the 55th throughout the war except for the period from January to June 1917 when he was detached to the Anzac Light Railways Unit.

On 29 September 1918 the main assault against the Hindenburg line commenced. The 5th Division was to pass through the American 30th Division, which was to take the first objective. While the American 30th Division was more successful in penetrating the defences than the American 27th Division, which also attacked that day, both were withdrawn and the attack continued with the Australian divisions. The Australians followed up and in the early part of October forced their way to the Beaurevoir line, the last of the Hindenburg defences.

The exploit for which Ryan was awarded the Victoria Cross occurred on 30 September when the 55th Battalion supported an attack near Bellicourt. In the initial assault Ryan was one of the first to reach the enemy's defences and his actions inspired others to overcome the garrison. When the Germans launched a strong and determined counter-attack Ryan organized and led a party of men in a bomb and bayonet charge against a party of enemy bombers who had infiltrated the rear of the position. Ryan's small party succeeded in killing the first three Germans encountered and then Ryan rushed the remainder with bombs and drove them back across no man's land. His action enabled the attack to be broken and the trench was retaken.

In this action Ryan was wounded in the shoulder and did not rejoin his unit until early December. He received the Victoria Cross from

King George V at Buckingham Palace on 22 May 1919. He was soon back in hospital, and he returned to Australia in September and was discharged in Sydney on 10 January 1920.

After the war Ryan had much trouble finding work and he roved through New South Wales and Victoria seeking employment. In 1935 he was employed by an insurance company in Melbourne.

Ryan died, impoverished, of pneumonia in Royal Melbourne Hospital on 3 June 1941 and was accorded a full military funeral. He was buried in the Roman Catholic section of Springvale cemetery and the memorial headstone was paid for by the Victorian government. His name is also commemorated on a plaque in the Victoria Garden of Remembrance at Springvale war cemetery. He was survived by two brothers and a sister. His sister, on 8 November 1967, presented his Victoria Cross to the Australian War Memorial and it is now housed there in the Hall of Valour.

SADLIER Clifford William King

RANK	Lieutenant
UNIT	51st Battalion, 13th Brigade, 4th Division
DATE	24–25 April 1918
PLACE	Villers-Bretonneux, France

CLIFFORD SADLIER was born at Camberwell, Victoria, on 11 June 1892, son of Thomas George Sadlier. He was educated at University High School, Melbourne, and in his youth went with his parents to Subiaco, Western Australia. He became a commercial traveller and was employed as such when he enlisted at Perth on 31 May 1915. Posted to the Australian Army Medical Corps, Sadlier was allocated to the 1st Australian General Hospital with which he served at Heliopolis, Egypt. He returned to Australia in February 1916 on nursing duty and on 9 November re-embarked as a reinforcement to the 51st Battalion.

Shortly after joining the unit on 18 May 1917 he was promoted to corporal, and on 14 July was appointed second lieutenant; promotion to lieutenant came on 1 April 1918.

On 24 April 1918 the Germans made their last lunge towards Amiens when they succeeded in capturing Villers-Bretonneux, Abbey Wood and part of Hangard Wood. A counter-attack was organized with the 15th Brigade, 5th Australian Division, attacking as the northern pincer to link up with the 13th Brigade, 4th Australian Division, which was attacking as the southern pincer. As the 13th Brigade assembled at 10 p.m. it was seen and fired upon from Abbey Wood. Sadlier, although wounded in the thigh, collected the members of his bombing section and with the support of Sergeant C.A. Stokes led them against the machine-guns, successfully killing the crews and capturing two guns. Sadlier alone attacked a third enemy machine-gun with his revolver, killing the crew of four and taking the gun. He was again wounded and forced to the rear. Stokes and the remaining men carried on and silenced all the guns along the wood. The whole southern pincer was able to sweep forward in time and link up with the 15th Brigade later in the morning. Both Stokes and Sadlier were recommended for the Victoria Cross but only one was awarded by higher authority; Stokes received the Distinguished Conduct Medal. Sadlier was decorated by King George V at Buckingham Palace on 17 July 1918.

Sadlier's wounds ended his active service and on 24 October he was invalided to Australia where his AIF appointment was terminated on 4 March 1919. On 1 January 1920 he was appointed lieutenant in the AMF and he was placed on the retired list on 1 September 1927.

He returned to Western Australia and for some time was state secretary of the Returned Soldiers', Sailors' and Airmen's Imperial League of Australia. He resigned to enter private business and later worked for the Repatriation Department in Perth. He attended the 1956 Victoria Cross centenary celebrations in London. Sadlier was a resident of Busselton, Western Australia, at the time of his death at Busselton District Hospital on 28 April 1964. He was accorded a full military funeral attended by over seventy ex-soldiers from the 51st Battalion. He was cremated and his ashes were interred at Karrakatta cemetery, Perth.

In 1933 Sadlier divorced his first wife and on 17 July 1936 married Alice Edith Smart.

SHOUT Alfred John

RANK	Captain
UNIT	1st Battalion, 1st Brigade, 1st Division
DATE	9 August 1915
PLACE	Lone Pine trenches, Gallipoli Peninsula, Turkey

A.J. SHOUT was born in New Zealand on 8 August 1882 to John Richard and Agnes Mary Shout. He was educated privately and at the age of eighteen went to South Africa with the New Zealand contingent. He attained the rank of sergeant and later served with the Cape Field Artillery from 1903 to 1907. He emigrated to Australia and worked as a carpenter and joiner, living in the Sydney suburb of Darlington. He joined the 29th Infantry Regiment of the militia in 1907 and was commissioned second lieutenant in that unit on 16 June 1914. He had married Rose Alice before he enlisted in the AIF. On 27 August 1914 he enlisted and was appointed to the 1st Battalion as second lieutenant and on 18 October embarked with his unit aboard A19 (SS *Afric*) for Egypt.

Shout, promoted to lieutenant on 1 February 1915, distinguished himself both at the landing at Gallipoli on 25 April and during the next ten days. He was twice wounded in action, on 27 April and 11 May, before he performed the action for which he was awarded the Victoria Cross. For displaying conspicuous courage and ability in organizing and leading his men in the thick, bushy country under withering fire, exposing himself repeatedly to locate the enemy, and leading a bayonet charge on Turkish positions, he was awarded the Military Cross and mentioned in General Sir Ian Hamilton's dispatches of 29 June. On 29 July he was promoted to captain.

On 6 August, at 5.40 p.m., at the commencement of the battle of Lone Pine, Shout's battalion attacked the Turkish trenches. The battalion had to beat off heavy counter-attacks the next day and was briefly withdrawn at 11.30 a.m. By 3 p.m. the battalion was back in the line repelling fierce attacks. These were defeated and there was a brief respite until 4.30 a.m. on the 8th. From then the unit fought continuously until 2 p.m. when it was relieved for a second time by the 7th Battalion. Early on the 9th the 1st Battalion re-entered Lone Pine and Shout performed the act at Sasse's sap for which he was awarded the Victoria Cross.

As a large portion of Sasse's sap was found to be occupied by the enemy, Captains Shout and Sasse decided to clear it. They gathered together three men carrying sandbags with which to construct barricades and then both officers charged down the trench, Shout bombing and Sasse shooting. They advanced in short 'hops', building a barricade at each stop. In the morning in one section of trench Shout killed eight enemy and routed the remainder. In the afternoon, gathering another party of eight and again accompanied by Sasse, he captured a further section of trench in similar fashion. They had just determined a suitable position for the final barricade when Shout lit three bombs for the final dash. The third bomb burst in his hand, blowing it completely away and shattering one side of his face and body. He was evacuated immediately but died of wounds aboard the hospital ship on 11 August. He was buried at sea.

After the war the citizens of Darlington commemorated the name of Alfred Shout on a memorial plaque which is now displayed at Victoria Barracks Museum, Paddington. His name is also commemorated on the Lone Pine Memorial.

STATTON Percy Clyde

RANK Sergeant
UNIT 40th Battalion, 10th Brigade, 3rd Division
DATE 12 August 1918
PLACE Near Proyart, France

PERCY STATTON was born at Beaconsfield, Tasmania, on 21 October 1890, the son of Edward Statton. He was educated at Zeehan state school and at the time of his enlistment on 1 March 1916 was farming at Tyenna, and had married Elsie May. He was posted to the 40th Battalion, embarked with that unit in July, and after a period of training in Britain, landed at Le Havre, France, in November.

Statton was appointed lance corporal on 22 May 1916 and promoted to corporal on 19 November. He was made temporary sergeant on 16 January 1917 and confirmed in that rank on 23 April.

During three days, 7–9 June, at Messines, he performed exceptionally fine service, under heavy artillery and machine-gun fire, in supervising and conducting carrying parties to troops in the front line. Several times these parties were decimated by shell-fire. His actions earned him the Military Medal. In October he was wounded and on 10 June 1918 was gassed in the Villers-Bretonneux area.

On 12 August 1918, the day Statton earned his Victoria Cross, the 40th Battalion was assigned an objective south of the Proyart–Chuignes road which entailed an advance of over 1300 metres. By 8.30 a.m. the 40th had successfully advanced 800 metres but were prevented from moving further forward by an intense artillery barrage. 'A' Company of the 40th, however, managed to reach the centre of Proyart village and with the aid of Statton's accurate Lewis gun fire advanced the full distance to its objective. The remainder of the battalion was able to follow. At about 6 p.m. the advance of the 37th Battalion, on the left flank, was held up by machine-gun fire. A party of thirteen men sent against the first enemy gun was virtually wiped out.

Statton supported the 37th's attack with two Lewis guns. When he saw the attack fail he got three men to follow him and, working along the bank of the Chuignes road, got to within seventy-five metres of the strong point. Statton, revolver in hand, then led his men across the seventy-five metres of open ground into the German trench. The party disposed of two guns and their crews and, at the second gun, Statton shot the whole crew, except one, with his revolver. As he had expended all his ammunition he had to grab the remaining German's rifle and use it to bayonet him. The small party then dashed towards the next two guns. The enemy retired only to be killed by the two Lewis guns Statton had sited earlier. Another enemy gun opened fire killing one member of the party and wounding another. Statton and the third man crawled back to their own lines as the 37th moved forward. That night he went out and brought in the wounded man and the body of the other.

Statton was presented with his Victoria Cross by King George V on 7 June 1919 at Buckingham Palace. In October he returned to Australia and on 18 January 1920 he was discharged in Tasmania. For several years he lived in Fitzgerald and worked in the timber industry. During bushfires in the Derwent Valley in 1934 Statton performed valuable rescue work in aiding families cut off by fire. In 1956 he attended the Victoria Cross centenary celebrations in London.

In his last years he lived at Ouse (formerly Brighton) where he was a member of the local council. He died in the Repatriation General Hospital, Hobart, on 7 December 1959, and was accorded a full military funeral. He was cremated and his ashes interred at Cornelian Bay cemetery in Hobart.

He was survived by his widow, Monica, who remarried, and a son. In 1968 his widow presented his medals to the Tasmania Command Headquarters Sergeants' Mess.

STORKEY Percy Valentine

RANK Lieutenant
UNIT 19th Battalion, 5th Brigade, 2nd Division
DATE 7 April 1918
PLACE Hangard Wood, France

PERCY STORKEY was born at Napier, Hawkes Bay, New Zealand, on 9 September 1891, son of Samuel James and Sarah Edith Storkey. He was educated at Napier high school, of which he was dux in 1910, and Victoria College, Wellington, where he studied first-year Arts. In 1911 he moved to Sydney, worked for a time in the office of a steamship company, then joined the administrative staff of the University of Sydney and enrolled in the law school.

He enlisted in the AIF on 10 May 1915 and his five years' previous service with the Wellington Infantry contributed to his being commissioned second lieutenant on 24 September. He sailed from Australia on 23 December as a reinforcement officer to the 19th Battalion. On 14 November 1916 he joined his unit in France. On the first day with his battalion he was wounded during an attack on Gird trenches, north of Flers. On 1 January 1917 he was promoted to lieutenant and on 10 October was again wounded when his battalion was engaged in the third battle of Ypres.

Storkey won his Victoria Cross at Hangard Wood, about 2000 metres south of Villers-Bretonneux. On this occasion two companies from the 19th and 20th Battalions were ordered to push through Hangard Wood and dig in along a road that skirted its western side. Both companies were very tired and, while waiting for the order to attack, some of the men, including Storkey, dozed off. He roused himself and to his surprise found that his men were seventy-five metres in front of him; he rejoined them. About a quarter of them were wounded as they pushed through the wood, including Storkey's company commander. When he emerged from the wood with six other men Storkey noticed that a large enemy party, about eighty to a hundred strong and armed with several machine-guns, was holding up the advance of troops on the right. He was joined by another officer and four men and under his leadership this party of twelve charged the enemy position with bayonets fixed. They drove the much larger enemy force out, killing or wounding thirty, and capturing three officers, fifty men and a machine-gun. Storkey pushed on to the objective, but that night the remnants of the two attacking companies withdrew to their unit areas.

The following month Storkey was appointed temporary company commander and temporary captain; on 10 June he was confirmed in this rank.

Storkey returned to Australia on 26 November and his AIF appointment ended on 31 January 1919; he was allocated to the reserve of officers on 1 July 1920. He resumed his studies at Sydney University and passed his final examinations while an associate to Mr Justice Wade of the Supreme Court. He was admitted to the bar on 8 June 1921. After a period in private practice Storkey was appointed to the New South Wales Department of Justice as crown prosecutor for the southwestern circuit, which covered the area bounded by Goulburn, Albury, Deniliquin, Hay, Wyalong and Broken Hill. On 15 April 1922 he married Molly M. Burnett.

Storkey was an active member of the Returned Services League and was first president of the Vaucluse sub-branch. Storkey served for one year in the Army Legal Department from October 1938 until June 1939. In May 1939 he was elevated to the New South Wales District Court Bench and was judge of the northern district until his retirement in December 1955. He moved to Teddington, Middlesex, UK, after retirement and died there on 3 October 1969.

His Victoria Cross was bequeathed to his old school, Napier Boys' High, and the machine-gun captured in the charge which he led is in the collection of the Australian War Memorial. A portrait by Max Meldrum hangs in the Archives Building, Wellington, New Zealand.

SYMONS William John

RANK   Lieutenant
UNIT   7th Battalion, 2nd Brigade, 1st Division
DATE   8–9 August 1915
PLACE   Lone Pine trenches, Gallipoli Peninsula, Turkey

WILLIAM SYMONS was born at Eaglehawk, Bendigo, Victoria, on 10 July 1889, to William Samson and Mary E. Symons. He was educated at Eaglehawk state school and became a commercial traveller residing at Brunswick, Melbourne. After serving for five years with the 5th

Battalion and three years in the 60th Battalion he enlisted in the AIF on 17 August 1914 and the following day was posted as colour sergeant to the 7th Battalion. He embarked with his unit on 18 October and landed at Gallipoli with it on 25 April 1915. A few days before the landing he had been appointed temporary regimental quartermaster sergeant and on the day following he was commissioned second lieutenant. Promotion to lieutenant came on 2 July and to captain on 1 May 1916.

On the night of 8–9 August 1915 Symons won his Victoria Cross. Symons was in command of the right section of the newly captured trenches held by his battalion and repelled several counter-attacks with great coolness. At about 5 a.m. on 9 August the Turks made a series of determined attacks on an isolated sap known as Jacob's trench. Six officers were, in succession, killed or severely wounded in the sap and a portion of it was lost. Symons was then instructed by Lieutenant Colonel H.E. Elliott to retake the sap. Symons organized and led a charge which drove the Turks out. He then rebuilt the barricade. He killed two of the enemy with his revolver. Then, when the sap was attacked from the front and two flanks, he obtained permission from Elliott to withdraw to adjacent overhead cover, leaving fifteen metres of open trench to the enemy, so that another barricade could be erected. The Turks persisted in the attack and twice fired the barricade woodwork but Symons led rushes that drove them back and the fires were extinguished. Eventu-

ally the Turks abandoned their attempt to take the sap.

Symons returned to Australia in March 1916 and was given a civic reception by the citizens of Brunswick. On 3 June he embarked as a company commander with the 37th Battalion and remained with that unit until the end of the war. He was mentioned in dispatches for his work during the big raid by the 10th Brigade near Armentières on 27 February 1917. He was badly gassed in France on 7 June 1917.

He married Isobel Anna Hockley at St Mary's Church, Hayling Island, Hampshire, UK, on 15 August 1918, the day before he left for Australia; there were three daughters of the marriage.

After returning to Australia, via Vancouver, on 10 November, his AIF appointment was terminated on 7 December. He saw service as a captain in the 2nd Battalion, 59th Infantry Regiment (later the 59th Battalion) prior to being transferred to the reserve of officers on 1 July 1922. Symons then returned to Britain and settled at Kenton, Hayling Island, and in time became a director of various firms and of stadiums. Symons joined the British Home Guard during the 1939–45 war and he was given the command of the 12th Battalion, Leicestershire Home Guard, with the rank of lieutenant colonel, an appointment he held for four years. For his military services he was made a Member of the Order of the British Empire in the New Year's list, 1944. He was for five years a member of the Leicestershire Military Interviewing Board as

Northern Command representative. He died in London on 24 June 1948. In December 1967, his widow put up his Victoria Cross and other service medals at public auction where they were bought by a London medal dealer for £800. The Returned Services League organized a successful public appeal for funds to buy the medals from the dealer and then donated the medals to the Australian War Memorial where they are displayed in the Hall of Valour.

THROSSELL Hugo Vivian Hope

RANK Second Lieutenant

UNIT 10th Light Horse Regiment, 3rd Light Horse Brigade, New Zealand and Australian Division

DATE 29–30 August 1915

PLACE Kaiakij Aghala (Hill 60), Gallipoli Peninsula, Turkey

HUGO THROSSELL was born at Northam, Western Australia, on 27 October 1884, the son of George (second premier of Western Australia) and Annie Throssell. He was educated at Prince Alfred College, Adelaide, and then returned to Western Australia to farm at Cowcowing. He enlisted in the AIF on 29 September 1914 and was posted to the state's first mounted squadron, which was later designated the 10th Light Horse Regiment. His six years' prior service with the 18th and

10th Regiments of the citizen forces contributed to his rapid promotion to sergeant on 6 October and his commissioning to second lieutenant on 3 February 1915.

Throssell did not embark with his unit, the 10th Light Horse, but joined it on Gallipoli two days before the fierce fighting at Walker's Ridge early on 7 August. On that day the 3rd Light Horse Brigade faced the heaviest fire encountered by the AIF when four lines of the 8th and 10th Light Horse Regiments charged towards the Turkish positions at the Nek. Throssell went over the top with the fourth wave which had seen three other waves cut to pieces. Throssell managed to get through the day unscathed.

Throssell's second major experience of action was during the fighting for the tactically important Hill 60 (Kaiakij Aghala) in late August. The hill was first attacked by the Australians on 21 August and a tenuous foothold was gained. It was attacked again on the 27th. The summit was gained but the Turks counter-attacked and retook the positions. At 10 p.m. on 28 August, the 10th Regiment was ordered to attack, capture and hold the enemy trenches. The attack commenced at 1 a.m. on the 29th and within seconds the light horsemen were engaged in furious hand-to-hand fighting in the Turkish trenches. They succeeded in driving the defenders back. About thirty minutes later, during consolidation, the Turks counter-attacked and overwhelmed the barricade in the trench. They were driven back. They attacked again at 3 a.m. on the

30th and a bloody fight took place. Despite appalling odds the 10th fought the Turks out of the trench back to their own lines. Just before daylight another attack was beaten back and at dawn the counter-attacks ceased. Reinforcements were brought in and consolidation went ahead.

Throssell was awarded the Victoria Cross for his bravery and devotion to duty in the battle for Hill 60. Despite his terrible wounds he refused to leave his post to obtain medical assistance until all danger had passed. When he had had his wounds dressed he returned to the firing line until ordered out of action by the medical officer. His wounds necessitated his hospitalization in Britain during which he contracted cerebro-spinal meningitis. In April 1916 he was invalided to Australia and allotted to 'light duties'. However, he worked tirelessly for the recruiting campaign. Earlier, on 20 February, he had been promoted to lieutenant.

Throssell took charge of light horse reinforcements on 22 January 1917 and by April was back with his unit for the second battle of Gaza. On 19 April his brother Frank was killed in action and Hugo was again wounded. He rejoined the 10th after recovery in December and served with it in the operations which culminated in the capture of Jerusalem. He had been promoted to captain on 15 August 1917. When General E. H. Allenby made his formal entry into Jerusalem through the Jaffa Gate on 10 December 1917, Throssell commanded the Australian detachment of the ceremonial guard.

In early 1918 Throssell was involved in training appointments, but his health broke down again and he returned to Australia. His AIF appointment was terminated on 13 February 1919. Later that year he married the novelist Katharine Susannah Prichard; they had one son. Throssell was appointed a member of the Soldier Settlers' Board, attached to the Department of Agriculture, but subsequently resigned to develop his own property at Greenmount. He had rejoined the department as an inspector a short time before he tragically committed suicide at his Lazy Hit Ranch, Greenmount, on 19 November 1933. He was buried in the Anglican section of the Karrakatta cemetery, Perth.

A memorial plaque was unveiled at Greenmount on 25 February 1954. The Australian War Memorial has a drawing of him by George Lambert. Streets in Greenmount and Melbourne are named after him.

Throssell's Victoria Cross and other service medals were donated to the People for Nuclear Disarmament in 1984. The Returned Services League purchased the medals and donated them to the Australian War Memorial where they are now displayed in the Hall of Valour.

TOWNER Edgar Thomas

RANK	Lieutenant
UNIT	2nd Machine Gun Battalion, 2nd Division
DATE	1 September 1918
PLACE	Mont St Quentin, north of Péronne, France

EDGAR TOWNER was born at Glencoe Station near Blackall, on the Barcoo River, Queensland, on 19 April 1890 to E.T. and Greta Towner. He was educated at Blackall state school and privately. He worked on his father's property until his enlistment on 4 January 1915. Allotted to the 7th reinforcements to the 25th Battalion he embarked with his unit in June; on 1 February 1916 he was promoted to sergeant. In March his unit sailed from Egypt to France where Towner served with the 25th until appointed second lieutenant on 18 November. He was then posted to 7th Company, 2nd Machine Gun Battalion, and on 24 February 1917 was promoted to lieutenant.

When Towner won his Victoria Cross during the attack on Mont St Quentin on 1 September 1918 the No. 3 Section, 7th Machine Gun Company, which he commanded, was attached to the 24th Battalion. The 24th's principal objective was the summit of the mount, and to reach it the battalion had to push through the village of Feuillaucourt and across the main road. The attack commenced at 6 a.m. and half an hour later enemy resistance was such that the whole advance was halted. During the early stages Towner had located and captured, single-handed, an enemy machine-gun. When the Germans were observed massing a stronger force for a counter-attack, Towner and his men got forward with two Vickers guns and the captured gun and produced such effective fire that the Germans suffered heavy losses. Later, by the skilful tactical placement of his guns, he cut off and captured twenty-five Germans. When the advance resumed Towner, despite heavy fire, would reconnoitre the best locations from which his guns could fire on the groups of enemy. When short of ammunition he secured an enemy machine-gun which, in full view of the Germans, he mounted and fired so effectively that the enemy retired, thus enabling the Australians to advance. At the critical time when the soldiers of the 21st Battalion attacked the heavily fortified crater on the summit objective Towner, although wounded, provided enfilade fire. With the crater lost, the enemy broke and Mont St Quentin passed into Australian hands.

The following night Towner was in command of a small detached post. He personally reconnoitred the enemy movements, but was evacuated exhausted thirty hours after being wounded.

Prior to winning the Victoria Cross Towner had won the Military Cross, on the night of 10–11 June 1918 south of Morlancourt, near Albert, for getting his guns into action and assisting the infantry to consolidate. He also utilized another captured machine-gun to advantage and, when an infantry post was blown in, he went out at great risk to himself and reorganized it. On 3 March 1917 and 4 March 1918 he was mentioned in dispatches.

King George V presented the Victoria Cross to him at Buckingham Palace on 10 April 1919 and on the 30th he returned to Australia where his AIF appointment was terminated on 16 August. He returned to Queensland and took up a grazing property, Kaloola, near Longreach. He also became a director and partner of the Rursleigh Pastoral Company.

Towner was appointed as a captain in the 26th Battalion of the Citizen Military Forces on 8 August 1939. After a period as company commander he became second-in-command, with the rank of temporary major, of the 26th of which H.W. Murray [q.v.] was commanding officer. He retired on 21 February 1942.

Towner was especially interested in geography and the explorations of Sir Thomas Mitchell. A fellow of the Royal Geographical Society of Australia and a member of the Royal Historical Society of New South Wales, in 1956 he received the Dr Thomson Foundation Gold Medal for his own geographical work.

He died on 27 August 1972 and was buried in Longreach, Queensland. He had not married. His medals were sold at auction in Sydney in 1983.

TUBB Frederick Harold

RANK	Captain
UNIT	7th Battalion, 2nd Brigade, 1st Division
DATE	9 August 1915
PLACE	Lone Pine trenches, Gallipoli Peninsula, Turkey

'FRED' TUBB was born at St Helena, Longwood, Victoria, on 28 November 1881, to Harry and Emma Tubb. He was educated at the East Longwood state school and became manager of his father's grazing property while also managing his own farm. He was at one time secretary of the local Mechanics' Institute and a member of the gun club and tennis club. Tubb had extensive militia experience. On 20 June 1900 he joined the Victorian Mounted Rifles and when the Commonwealth Light Horse was founded he transferred to it and served in that unit until 1911; he attained the rank of sergeant. When compulsory service came into force, Tubb, in November 1911, transferred to the 60th Infantry Battalion; he was commissioned second lieutenant on 2 December 1912. On 1 July 1913 he again transferred, this time to the newly formed 58th Infantry Battalion (Essendon Rifles).

He enlisted in the AIF on 24 August 1914 and was appointed a second lieutenant in the newly raised 7th Battalion. On 1 February 1915 he was promoted to lieutenant and on 6 August that year became a captain, three days before winning the Victoria Cross. During the Turkish counter-attack on 9 August Tubb was in command of a section of trench which was the scene of some intense fighting. When the enemy blew in a sandbag barricade Tubb led his men back, repulsed the enemy and had the barricade rebuilt. The enemy attacked and again twice blew in the barricades, but Tubb, bleeding from bomb wounds in the arm and scalp, continued to fight. Supported by Corporals Dunstan [q.v.] and Burton [q.v.], he succeeded in rebuilding the barricade. A bomb blast killed Burton and wounded Dunstan. Tubb obtained further men from the next post, Tubb's Corner. The enemy attack had weakened, however, and although heavy bombing continued the position was held.

In 1916, after the evacuation of Anzac, Tubb visited Australia and was accorded a hero's welcome in Victoria. He returned to France and was promoted to major on 17 February 1917.

On 20 September 1917, the 7th Battalion fought in the first of the step-by-step battles known as the battle of Menin Road and which were part of the third battle of Ypres which had commenced on 31 July. The 5th and 6th Battalions took the first and second of the brigade objectives and at 9.53 a.m. the 7th Battalion advanced towards the third objective. Tubb's company seized a group of nine pillboxes which, according to the artillery map, were 250 metres short of the barrage. Part of the barrage fell on the company, hitting Tubb. He was evacuated but died that evening in a dressing station. He was buried in Lijessenthoek military cemetery, Poperinghe, Belgium.

An elder brother, Captain Frank Reid Tubb, who had served in South Africa, also served throughout the 1914–18 war with the 7th Battalion and gained a Military Cross. Two other brothers also served in the AIF.

At Euroa, in December 1936, Tubb was commemorated in the Avenue of Honour and a nearby hill was named Tubb Hill after him. His Victoria Cross is displayed in the Australian War Memorial's Hall of Valour.

WARK Blair Anderson

RANK	Major
UNIT	32nd Battalion, 8th Brigade, 5th Division
DATE	29 September – 1 October 1918
PLACE	Bellicourt to Joncourt, France

BLAIR WARK was born at Bathurst, New South Wales, on 27 July 1894 to Alexander and Blanche Adelaide Wark. He was educated at the Fairleigh Grammar School, Bathurst, then Sydney Technical College, where he studied quantity surveying.

From July 1911 to July 1912 Wark served as a senior cadet and attained the rank of sergeant. He then joined the 18th North Sydney Infantry, was promoted to corporal in 1913 and appointed second lieutenant on 16 August of that year; at the commencement of war he was on full-time duty for the defence of the port of Sydney.

Wark enlisted in the AIF on 5 August 1915 and was posted as a lieutenant to the 30th Battalion. He then attended an infantry school at Liverpool, completed a short course at Duntroon, and embarked for Egypt in November 1915 where he served on the Canal defences. In June 1916 he sailed for France and was there wounded in the battle of Fromelles on 19 July; he had been promoted to lieutenant on 5 August 1915 and captain on 20 February 1916. Wark returned to France after recovering from his wound and transferred to the 32nd Battalion on 18 November. On 27 April 1917 he received his majority and was temporarily second-in-command of the unit. During the third battle of Ypres, at Polygon Wood in 1917, Wark, then a company commander, won the Distinguished Service Order. The enemy massed to counter-attack his company position on three occasions but were, each time, repulsed. He sent out patrols which thwarted another attack and his courage and devotion to duty were an inspiration to all.

Wark went to Aldershot, UK, in January 1918 to undertake a senior officers' course. He returned in March to become battalion second-in-command. He actually commanded the battalion in its fights of June and July and through the final offensives; he was mentioned in dispatches in June.

On 29 September 1918 the main assault against the Hindenburg line commenced. The 5th Australian Division was to pass through the American 30th Division after it had captured its first objective. Wark was in command of the 32nd Battalion which crossed the start line at 9 a.m. moving south of Bellicourt. When the advance was held up by two machine-guns he employed a passing tank to deal with them. He then gathered together 200 leaderless Americans and attached them to his own command. With the support of tanks his men swept through Nauroy at 11.30 a.m. taking forty prisoners. When he observed a battery of 77 mm guns firing on his rear companies and causing heavy casualties, Wark collected a few men and rushed the battery, capturing four guns and ten of the crew. With only two non-commissioned officers he pushed forward and surprised and captured fifty Germans near Magny-la-Fosse. At about 3 p.m. Wark halted his troops near Joncourt. Patrols found the town occupied, and so the 32nd withdrew slightly. However they were in position in time to repel a counter-attack by 400 Germans at 5.30 p.m.

At 7 a.m. next day the unit attacked again and advanced 1500 metres to a point just north of Etricourt. Another attack took place at 6 a.m. on 1 October and the troops pushed through Joncourt and beyond. Wark's gallantry was often exhibited as he again led from the front. Regardless of personal risk he dashed forward and silenced machine-guns which were causing heavy casualties. This and other successes enabled the division to complete its task of forcing through to the Beaurevoir line. For his bravery, initiative and control Wark was awarded the Victoria Cross.

Wark's appointment was terminated on 28 September 1919 and he resumed his business as a quantity surveyor in Sydney. He was active in public life. He was variously a director of the Royal North Shore Hospital, life governor of the New South Wales Benevolent Society, a councillor of the New South Wales National Roads and Motorists' Association, a committee member of the Hawkesbury Race Club and a director of insurance and petroleum companies.

He was twice married, first to Phyllis Marquiss-Munro on 31 May 1912 at St George's Parish Church, Worthing, UK, and then to Katherine Mary Davis. He had one son and two daughters.

On 17 April 1940 Wark was appointed to the 1st Battalion (the City of Sydney's Own Regiment) as a major. On 26 July he was promoted to temporary lieutenant colonel and appointed to command the regiment. He died suddenly at Puckapunyal Camp, Victoria, on 13 June 1941 and his ashes were interred at Woronora cemetery, Sydney. His name is commemorated on a plaque at the New South Wales Garden of Remembrance, Rookwood war cemetery.

His second wife attended the Victoria Cross centenary celebrations in London in 1956. The Australian War Memorial has on display one of the 77 mm guns that he captured.

WEATHERS Lawrence Carthage

RANK	Temporary Corporal
UNIT	43rd Battalion, 11th Brigade, 3rd Division
DATE	2 September 1918
PLACE	North of Péronne, France

LAWRENCE WEATHERS was born at Te Koparu, New Zealand, on 14 May 1890, to John Joseph and Ellen Frances Johanna Weathers. At the age of seven he moved to Australia with his parents and settled in Adelaide. He was educated at Snowtown public school and at the time of his enlistment on 3 February 1916 was an undertaker, married, and living in Parkside.

Weathers embarked on 9 June, was taken on strength of the 43rd Battalion in November, and after training in Britain moved to France in November. From January to April 1917 he was hospitalized. On 10 June, during a night operation at Messines, he was severely wounded and did not rejoin his unit until the end of the year. He was appointed lance corporal on 21 March 1918. On 26 May 1918 Weathers was gassed but rejoined his unit a month later.

Mont St Quentin was captured by the 2nd Division on 1 September and next day the division continued to advance in a north-easterly direction. The 74th British Division was advancing in an easterly direction leaving the 43rd Battalion, the only battalion of the 3rd Division still in the line, to clear a small triangle of ground near Allaines. Their task on 2 September was that of clearing two objectives — Graz trench, opposite Allaines, and Scutari trench to the north. A platoon from the 41st Battalion and D Company of the 43rd first cleared Scutari trench. The enemy were then hemmed in by A and B Companies moving from the south, and C and D Companies moving from the north. At this stage, with the enemy concentrated into a fork of the trenches, and the two prongs closing in, the Germans checked the Australian advance with a great volume of fire. Weathers then rushed in and bombed the Germans, killing the garrison's leader. He came back for more bombs and went out with three comrades, including a Lewis gunner. As the Lewis gun covered him he ran to the enemy parapet and bombed the trench, and with the support of his three comrades and the commander of the attached 41st platoon, captured 180 prisoners and three machine-guns. By 7 a.m. the 43rd had occupied all its objectives. For his actions Weathers was awarded the Victoria Cross.

On the 28th the 43rd moved up to attack the Beaurevoir line. Weathers, mortally wounded by a shell burst in the subsequent attack on 29 September, was buried in Unicorn cemetery, Vendhuille, France. He was survived by his widow and a son. A brother, Trooper Thomas Francis Weathers, 9th Light Horse, had died of wounds on 15 June 1915 on Gallipoli.

WHITTLE John Woods

RANK	Sergeant
UNIT	12th Battalion, 3rd Brigade, 1st Division
DATE	8 April and 15 April 1917
PLACE	West of Boursies and Lagnicourt, France

JOHN WHITTLE was born at Huon Island, Tasmania, on 3 August 1883, son of Henry Whittle. He was living in Hobart when he enlisted in the Fourth (Second Imperial Bushmen) Contingent which embarked for South Africa on 27 March 1901. He returned to Australia on 25 June 1902 and shortly after enlisted in the Royal Navy, and served as a stoker for five years on various ships on the Australian Station. He returned to the army at the end of his navy service and variously served in the Army Service Corps, the 31st Battery and the Tasmanian Rifle Regiment.

Whittle enlisted in the AIF on 6

August 1915 and sailed as a reinforcement for the 26th Battalion. He was reallotted to the 12th in Egypt and taken on strength on 1 March. He was promoted to corporal on 14 March and a month after his arrival in France became lance sergeant. He was wounded on 18 July 1916, returned to his unit in October, and was promoted to sergeant on 14 October.

In February 1917, during the advance on Bapaume, he was with Captain Newland [q.v.] in the battalion's assault on the villages of Le Barque and Ligny-Thilloy. At Bark trench on the 27th, where Newland was wounded, Whittle was one of the first into the enemy trench and he bombed the enemy out. For his gallantry he was awarded the Distinguished Conduct Medal.

Whittle won his Victoria Cross at the same time as Newland, on the Bapaume–Cambrai road near Boursies, and at Lagnicourt during the period 8–15 April 1917. In the initial advances of Newland's A Company on Boursies, Whittle had charge of the left platoon. After a successful bombing assault on the ruined mill, Whittle was placed in command of a post just beyond it. Around 10 p.m. the Germans counter-attacked and succeeded in entering the small trench Whittle was holding. Whittle quickly reorganized his men, charged the enemy and restabilized the position. Newland then arrived and the two worked together until the line was re-established.

Later on the 15th at Lagnicourt, when the enemy counter-attacked and penetrated the D Company line

and worked in behind D and A Companies, Newland and Whittle again co-operated splendidly. Newland, under attack from three directions, withdrew his men to a sunken road and lined them out in defence along both banks. Just as this move was completed, Whittle, who had seen some Germans moving a machine-gun into a position which offered a commanding arc of fire, jumped to his feet and charged the enemy gun crew. He killed the whole crew and then carried the machine-gun back to the Australian positions. Newland then consolidated the position and when reinforcements from the 9th Battalion arrived a counter-attack was executed and all positions were regained.

Whittle received both his Victoria Cross and Distinguished Conduct Medal from King George V at an investiture held at Buckingham Palace on 21 July 1917. In March 1918 Whittle was wounded for the second time and in July he was again wounded and hospitalized. When he was discharged from hospital he returned to Australia to assist in the recruiting programme and was there when the war ended; he was discharged in Tasmania on 15 December.

In the 1920s he moved to Sydney and was for many years an inspector with a large insurance company. Whittle was responsible for saving the life of a three-year-old boy in 1934 when he rescued him from drowning. For this exploit he received a certificate of merit from the Royal Life Saving Society.

Whittle died on 2 March 1946 at

Glebe and was survived by his widow, Emily Margaret, a son and three daughters. He was buried at the Catholic cemetery, Rookwood. Another son was among many members of the 2/33rd Battalion killed in New Guinea in 1943 when a Liberator crashed into a marshalling park. Whittle's medals are in a private collection in Sydney.

WOODS James Park

RANK   Private
UNIT   48th Battalion, 12th Brigade, 4th Division
DATE   18 September 1918
PLACE   Near Le Verguier, north-west of St Quentin, France

'JIMMY' WOODS was born at Gawler, South Australia, on 2 January 1891. He was working as a vigneron at Caversham, Western Australia, at the time of his enlistment on 29 September 1916. He was posted as a reinforcement to the 48th Battalion, embarked in December and arrived in Britain in February 1917. After a period in hospital he sailed for France on 1 September and joined his unit on the 13th; in January and July 1918 he had two further periods in hospital.

Woods won his Victoria Cross during an advance towards the Hindenburg line by the 12th Brigade on 18 September 1918. His unit succeeded in capturing its first objective along with some 480 prisoners. The 45th Battalion then passed through and secured its objective and the 46th commenced its thrust to the final objective. On the right flank the British troops were held up before their second objective. A company of the 48th was sent to form a protecting flank for the right of the 46th, which temporarily held a position west of the brigade's final objective. The British commander several times reported that his troops were actually in position on Fourmi trench, but Woods and three companions conducted a patrol which proved him wrong.

The patrol found the enemy post to be strongly defended by the Germans and from it the enemy commanded excellent fields of fire. The position obviously required a concentrated attack, but while it was being organized Woods and his small party attacked it. Once in the position Woods killed one German and the rest, at least thirty, fled leaving four heavy and two light machine-guns. Although one of the small party was wounded the Australians held the trench against determined counter-attacks. Woods retaliated by climbing on to the parapet and lying there, throwing bombs passed up to him by his comrades. He kept this up until help arrived and the captured post was consolidated. The fight for the trench went on until dawn when the 48th ejected the enemy. The casualties, however, were high as the British division on the right flank was still 800 metres back.

Woods embarked for return to Australia on 21 June 1919 and was discharged from the AIF in Perth on 10 September. He had been invested with the Victoria Cross by King George V at Buckingham Palace on 31 May 1919. On 30 April 1922 he married Olive D. Wilson and their family consisted of three sons and three daughters.

He lived at Claremont, Western Australia, until his death on 18 January 1963. He was buried in the Methodist section of Karrakatta cemetery, Perth. He had attended the Victoria Cross centenary in London in 1956.

North Russia 1919

PEARSE Samuel George

RANK	Sergeant
UNIT	45th Battalion, Royal Fusiliers, Sadlier-Jackson's Brigade
DATE	29 August 1919
PLACE	North of Emtsa, north Russia

SAMUEL PEARSE was born at Penarth, Glamorganshire, UK, on 16 July 1897, to George Stapleton and Sarah Ann Pearse. He moved with his family to Australia where his father took up property at Koorlong, near Mildura in Victoria. He had served in the militia, in the 73rd Battalion, for two years when he enlisted in the AIF at Melbourne, stating his occupation as trapper, on 5 July 1915. He embarked for Egypt in September 1915 and was taken on the strength of the 7th Battalion at Gallipoli on 7 December. He transferred to the 2nd Machine Gun Company on 24 August 1916, was wounded the same day, but returned to his unit soon after.

On 28 September 1917 he was awarded the Military Medal for courage and resource during the fighting east of Ypres. While on outpost duty he crept forward and bombed a German post, causing casualties. The position was abandoned by the enemy. Later, while acting as a runner, he saved many lives by bringing in a wounded man on each occasion he made a 'run'. He was promoted to lance corporal on 21 November 1917 and to corporal on 10 April 1918. He was again wounded in action on 19 May 1918. After a period of training at the Machine Gun Depot he joined the 1st Machine Gun Battalion on 1 December.

Having volunteered for the North Russia Relief Force in 1919, he was discharged from the AIF in Britain on 18 July 1919 and went to Russia with the 45th Battalion, the Royal Fusiliers, almost immediately following his enlistment in the British army.

The attack launched by Brigadier General L.W. de V. Sadlier-Jackson on the Dvina River on 10 August was a success and allowed the British and Allied forces to withdraw without interference from the Bolsheviks. In addition to the forces on the Dvina River, elements of the Royal Fusiliers were operating about 160 kilometres south of Archangel along the railway. Pearse was killed during the final offensive action by the British along this railway.

On 29 August during an attack on an enemy battery position north of Emtsa, Pearse, under heavy enemy fire, cut his way through barbed wire thus clearing a way for troops to enter. Enemy fire from a blockhouse was causing casualties so Pearse charged single-handed, killing the occupants with bombs. He was killed by machine-gun fire several minutes later. It was largely due to Pearse that the position was carried with so few casualties. He was buried at Obozerskay which is on the railway line between Emtsa and Archangel. His name is commemorated in the Archangel war cemetery. Pearse was posthumously awarded the Victoria Cross, and his widow received the award from King George V at Buckingham Palace on 25 March 1920.

SULLIVAN Arthur Percy

RANK   Corporal
UNIT   45th Battalion, Royal Fusiliers, Sadlier-Jackson Brigade
DATE   10 August 1919
PLACE Dvina River, south of Archangel, north Russia

ARTHUR SULLIVAN was born at Crystal Brook, South Australia, on 27 November 1896, son of A.M. Sullivan. Following his schooling he joined the National Bank in 1913 at Gladstone, South Australia. He moved to Broken Hill, New South Wales, and later was stationed at Maitland, South Australia. He enlisted in the AIF at Port Pirie, South Australia, on 27 April 1918 and embarked on 23 July.

Initially allotted as a reinforcement to the 10th Battalion he was on 5 October posted as an artillery reinforcement. Sullivan was promoted to acting corporal on 23 March 1919.

The war was over before he was allotted to a unit in France. Sullivan, determined to see active service, volunteered for the British North Russia Relief Force. He was accordingly discharged from the AIF on 12 June and embarked with the force as a member of the 45th Battalion, the Royal Fusiliers.

In June and July 1919, the two brigades of the force disembarked in Archangel and relieved the original 1918 expeditionary force. L.W. de V. Sadlier-Jackson's brigade moved about 240 kilometres down the Dvina River to the front line. Although the decision had been made to withdraw the forces, Sadlier-Jackson attacked the Bolshevik positions on 10 August in order to gain time for the evacuation and to help the morale of the White Russian forces. It was here that Sullivan was awarded the Victoria Cross.

As Sullivan's platoon was crossing the river by means of a narrow plank, four of them, including an officer, fell off into a swamp. Without hesitation, and despite the intense fire they were under, Sullivan jumped in and rescued all four, bringing them out one by one. His exhausted comrades would undoubtedly have drowned without his assistance.

Upon his return to Britain Sullivan elected to return directly to Australia rather than wait in London for his Victoria Cross investiture. He received the medal from Edward, Prince of Wales, at Government House, Adelaide, on 12 July 1920, during the Prince's tour of Australia. He rejoined the National Bank, first at Maitland, then at Orroroo, South Australia. In 1929 he was transferred to head office in Sydney, and in July 1934 was appointed manager at Casino, New South Wales.

In 1937 Sullivan was selected to join the Australian military contingent to the coronation of King George VI, and was enlisted in the AMF. His first duty in Britain was to hand to relatives for burial the ashes of his friend Sergeant A. Evans, VC, DCM, of the Lincolnshire Regiment, who had died in Australia.

On 9 April 1937, not long after handing over the ashes, Sullivan was returning to his quarters at Wellington Barracks when he slipped and fell heavily against the gutter. At the same time a cyclist crashed into him. He was taken to hospital but died soon after from the blow to his head which he had received when he fell.

In London Sullivan was accorded a full military funeral. His ashes were returned to Sydney and placed at the Northern Suburbs Crematorium in July 1937. A bronze plaque, provided by members of the 1937 contingent, was later placed on the gates at Wellington Barracks near the spot where he was killed.

Sullivan was survived by his widow, Dorothy Frances, who attended the 1956 Victoria Cross centenary celebrations in London, and three children. The Victoria Cross of this shy and popular personality is displayed in the Australian War Memorial's Hall of Valour.

The 1939–45 war

ANDERSON Charles Groves Wright

RANK	Lieutenant Colonel
UNIT	2/19th Battalion, 22nd Brigade, 8th Division
DATE	18–22 January 1942
PLACE	Muar River, Malaya (now Malaysia)

C.G.W. ANDERSON was born at Cape Town, South Africa, on 12 February 1897. On 13 October 1916 he was commissioned as a lieutenant in the King's African Rifles and fought with its 3rd Battalion in East Africa against the German-led Askari. In addition to being awarded the Military Cross he gained valuable jungle warfare experience.

Anderson purchased a grazing property near Crowther, New South Wales, in 1934 and moved with his wife to Australia from Africa that year; he had married Edith M. Tout on 21 February 1931. On 3 March 1939 he joined the CMF and was appointed a captain in the 56th Battalion (Riverina Regiment). He was promoted to major on 26 October and on 1 July 1940 was seconded to the AIF as second-in-command of the 2/19th Battalion when the unit was formed at Wallgrove, New South Wales, in late July. After unit training at Wallgrove, Ingleburn and Bathurst, the 2/19th embarked for Malaya in February 1941. On 1 August 1941 he was promoted to lieutenant colonel and appointed to command the 2/19th.

Anderson was awarded his Victoria Cross during operations against the Japanese in Malaya in the period 18–22 January 1942. In mid-January in the Muar area the left flank of Westforce (four brigades) began to crumble when the Japanese *Guards Division*, which had joined the *5th Division* in western Malaya, attacked the inexperienced 45th Indian Brigade. The Guards crossed the Muar River and pressed on towards Bakri, situated at a junction on the road to Yong Peng. It encountered the 2/29th Battalion, which had reinforced the 45th Indian Brigade. Anderson's 2/19th, sent from Eastforce, arrived at Bakri on the morning of 18 January to reinforce the brigade. It soon became engaged with the Japanese who had come in at the rear of the 2/29th. At about 10 a.m. on 19 January, the headquarters of the 45th Indian Brigade was bombed, incapacitating Brigadier H.C. Duncan, the brigade commander, who with his brigade major were the only survivors of the headquarters staff.

Anderson then took command of the brigade which had one Indian battalion isolated and two other Indian battalions in disorder at Bakri. They had suffered heavy casualties. He waited until the afternoon before withdrawing the 2/29th into the Bakri perimeter, by which time 200 men of the isolated battalion had reached Australian lines. During this period, both the 2/19th and 2/29th were heavily engaged with the Japanese units which moved behind Bakri and held the road to Yong Peng.

On the morning of 20 January a fighting withdrawal to Parit Sulong, a vital bridge on the road to Yong Peng, began. The leading company broke through a Japanese force, but the main force were still hemmed in and vulnerable to air attack. Another company went into the attack singing 'Waltzing Matilda' with Anderson himself leading the final attack. He personally put two machine-gun posts out of action with grenades and shot two Japanese with his pistol.

Further on they encountered another roadblock and the Japanese, following close behind the Australian Indian column, pressed the rearguard until a counter-attack was launched in which Brigadier Duncan was killed. Meanwhile Anderson, with the advance guard, organized a three-company attack which put the enemy to flight. That night Anderson learnt that the Japanese were in Parit Sulong and his force was isolated. On 21 January Anderson's force encountered the Japanese strongly established around Parit Sulong. They attacked, but had gained only a few hundred metres by nightfall. Anderson's force now had

many wounded and its artillery and mortar ammunition was almost exhausted. A battalion of the Loyals was ordered to launch a relieving attack but this was delayed and eventually abandoned on 22 January. Early that morning Japanese tanks broke into the perimeter of Anderson's force from its rear, but were stopped by gunfire. The isolated force was bombed from the air and shelled by artillery, as it had been throughout its withdrawal. At 9 a.m. Anderson ordered that his vehicles and guns be destroyed and the men withdraw eastward in small parties. Anderson's force had done all that could reasonably have been expected, but their losses were heavy. The 45th Indian Brigade had been decimated, and the two Australian battalions had suffered heavily. Of the 2/19th only 271 men reached Yong Peng, of the 2/29th only 130.

On 15 February 1942 Anderson was taken into captivity when British forces in Malaya surrendered. He was released in August 1945 and repatriated to Australia where his AIF appointment was terminated on 21 December 1945. He was invested with the Victoria Cross by the Governor-General, the Duke of Gloucester, at Sydney on 8 January 1947.

He had returned to his property after the war, and in the general election of 1949 Anderson was elected to the House of Representatives as Country Party member for Hume, New South Wales. He was defeated in 1951, regained the seat in the 1955 elections, retained it in 1958, but was again defeated in December 1961. From 10 April 1957 until his defeat he served as a member of the joint committee on the Australian Capital Territory.

Anderson lives in Red Hill, Australian Capital Territory, and has a family of two daughters and twin sons. A portrait by J.B. Godson hangs in the Australian War Memorial's Hall of Valour.

CHOWNE Albert

RANK   Lieutenant
UNIT   2/2nd Battalion, 16th Brigade, 6th Division
DATE   25 March 1945
PLACE   Dagua, New Guinea (now Papua New Guinea)

'BERT' CHOWNE was born in Sydney, New South Wales, on 19 July 1920, son of A.J. Chowne. He was educated in the Willoughby area and was closely associated with the boy scouts and tennis and football clubs. He worked as a shirt cutter in the city and joined the 36th Battalion of the militia at Rutherford in January 1940. He enlisted in the AIF on 30 May 1940 and, after unsuccessfully attempting to join the 6th Division, was posted to the 2/13th Battalion. The battalion embarked in October and arrived in the Middle East on 26 November; it had initially been formed as part of the 7th Division but early in 1941 it was transferred to the 9th. Chowne served first as company runner and later as a member of the carrier platoon. From April to December he was part of the Tobruk garrison, then was assigned to garrison duty in Syria. He returned to the western desert in June 1942. He had been promoted to corporal on 21 April 1941 and to sergeant a year later.

At El Alamein his carrier, a light armoured vehicle with a mounted Bren gun, played a notable part in repelling the German attack below Trig 33 in September. On the night of 23 October he was employed as battalion liaison officer between his commanding officer and a British tank regiment. When his carrier was knocked out he continued as an infantryman until wounded on 24 October. After El Alamein he returned with his unit, via Palestine, to Australia.

In July 1943 Chowne, now mortar platoon sergeant, embarked with his unit for New Guinea. He fought at Lae, Finschhafen and Sattelberg. At Finschhafen, on 25 September, he gained a Military Medal when he crept close to Japanese lines dragging telephone lines behind him. He then brought down accurate mortar fire on the enemy positions.

Chowne next attended an officer cadet training unit and graduated after a course in which he came top of the tactical wing, second in the weapon wing and second in the school. He was commissioned lieutenant, infantry reinforcements, on 23 January 1944 and managed for two months to be posted to the 2/13th Battalion. Although his unit appealed to retain his services he was posted to the Jungle Warfare Centre, Canungra, Queensland, and thence, on 7 October, to the 2/2nd Battalion. He joined the 2/2nd at Atherton, Queensland, and went with that unit to Aitape, New Guinea, in December.

Chowne quickly established a reputation for courage and leadership. On 8 March he conducted a one-man patrol forward of the battalion patrol limits to the Ninahau River and brought back valuable information on the river, tracks and enemy. After the capture of Dagua the main enemy force withdrew southwards from the beach to previously prepared positions on the flank of the division. As the Japanese location hindered further movement towards Wewak the 2/2nd was ordered to destroy the enemy force.

On 25 March A Company, 2/2nd, attacked the position but the leading platoon came under heavy fire from concealed machine-guns sited on a small rise which dominated the approach to the positions. The enemy inflicted casualties, which included the platoon commander. Chowne saw their plight and rushed up the steep, narrow track and hurled grenades which knocked out two enemy light machine-guns. He called on his men to follow him, and firing his sub-machine-gun from the hip, charged the enemy. Although seriously wounded in the chest, his momentum carried him forward and he was able to kill two more Japanese before he himself was killed standing over three enemy foxholes. His actions contributed greatly to the capture of this heavily defended position (later renamed 'Chowne Knoll') and paved the way for the division's advance to Wewak. He was buried in Lae war cemetery and was posthumously awarded the Victoria Cross. It was the first awarded to the 6th Australian Division which had first gone into action at Bardia nearly four years earlier.

A street is named after Chowne in Campbell, Australian Capital Territory. On 3 July 1954 the Governor of New South Wales, Lieutenant General Sir John Northcott, officially opened the Lieutenant Albert Chowne Memorial Hall in Willoughby.

The Victoria Cross and Military Medal conferred upon Chowne were presented by the Governor-General, the Duke of Gloucester, to Chowne's young widow early in 1946. He had married Corporal Daphne May Barton, Australian Women's Army Service, on 15 May 1944. She later remarried and in 1981 presented Chowne's medals to the Australian War Memorial where they are now displayed in the Hall of Valour.

CUTLER Arthur Roden

RANK   Lieutenant
UNIT   2/5th Field Regiment,
         7th Division
DATE   19 June – 6 July 1941
PLACE Merdjayoun and
         Damour area, Lebanon

SIR RODEN CUTLER was born at Manly, New South Wales, on 24 May 1916, the son of Arthur William and Ruby Cutler. He was educated at Sydney high school and the University of Sydney. After graduating with a Bachelor of Economics in 1934 he joined the Public Trust Office of the New South Wales Justice Department. He joined the Sydney University Regiment while a student and on 10 November 1939 was commissioned lieutenant in the CMF.

On 1 May 1940 Cutler joined the AIF and was posted to the 2/5th Field Regiment of the 7th Divisional Artillery. His unit trained in New South Wales prior to its embarkation on 19 October. Training continued in Palestine and Egypt before the unit went into action in Syria in June 1941.

It was during the Syrian campaign that Cutler received his Victoria Cross for conspicuous and sustained gallantry over a period of eighteen days. He is the only Australian artilleryman to win the Victoria Cross.

At Merdjayoun, on 19 June, the Australian infantry attack had been checked by the enemy who had counter-attacked with tanks. The artillery forward observation team attached to the 2/25th Battalion, including Cutler, another officer, two gunners, and a few infantrymen, pushed on ahead of the main body and established an outpost in a house. Cutler then went out under intense machine-gun fire to repair the telephone line, and when this was done enemy posts and batteries were successfully engaged. The outpost was then attacked by two tanks and supporting infantry. Cutler and one of the gunners opened fire on the tracks of the tanks with anti-tank rifles, but to no great effect. The two men then exchanged their anti-tank rifles for a rifle and a Bren gun, driving the enemy infantry to cover. The tanks advanced again and opened fire with their turret guns. Cutler took up an anti-tank rifle and hit the tanks' turrets, but again without effect. Then he fired and hit their tracks, whereupon tanks and infantry withdrew to shelter. Covered by the fire of their own infantry, the surviving Australians withdrew and Cutler personally supervised the evacuation of the wounded.

Cutler was convinced that the enemy were unsure of themselves and that it would be wise to press on into the towns where the attackers could find shelter from the tanks. Although Merdjayoun was occupied by members of the Foreign Legion he established an observation post among rocks at the north-west corner of the town and registered the only road by which enemy transport could enter the town. The enemy counter-attacked with infantry and tanks and Cutler was cut off. After dark he succeeded in making his way through enemy lines. His registering of the road, however, was of vital importance and a big factor in the enemy's subsequent retreat.

On the night of 23–24 June Cutler was in charge of a 25-pounder field gun which he took forward to the defended localities. At dawn on the 24th he placed it in position in front of the infantry in order to fire on the French posts at point-blank range, and in particular at an enemy anti-tank gun and post. Later, at Damour on 6 July, again as an artillery observation officer but this time attached to the 2/16th Battalion, Cutler again became involved in the infantry fight and captured eight Frenchmen from three machine-gun posts. The infantry's wireless would not work in such hilly country and Cutler offered to carry a telephone line forward so that he could bring artillery fire down on the enemy posts. On the way he was severely wounded in the leg and he lay isolated and exposed for twenty-six hours before he was rescued. As his leg had become septic it was amputated when he reached the main dressing station.

Cutler was invalided home and retired from the AIF in December 1941. He received his Victoria Cross from the Governor-General, Lord Gowrie, VC, in Sydney on 11 June 1942. That year he was elected state secretary of the Returned Soldiers', Sailors' and Airmen's Imperial League of Australia. During his period with the league Cutler was also a member of the Aliens Classification and Advisory Committee which was set up to advise the Commonwealth government. In 1943 he was appointed assistant deputy director of the Security Service in New South Wales and later that year became an assistant commissioner in the Commonwealth Department of Repatriation.

Cutler left Australia in 1946 to become Australian High Commissioner to New Zealand. He returned in 1952 and for the next three years was High Commissioner in Ceylon. In June 1955 he was appointed Australian Minister to Egypt, but in November 1956 he returned to Australia because of the Suez crisis; he was made CBE in January 1957.

Back in Australia, Cutler acted as secretary-general of the SEATO Council of Foreign Ministers held in Canberra in January 1957, and in August 1958 was elected president of the Australian Capital Territory branch of the Returned Services League. That same month he was appointed High Commissioner for Australia in Pakistan, and in July 1961 became Australian Consul-General in New York. Prior to the latter two diplomatic appointments he had been chief of protocol in the Department of External Affairs.

In September 1965 Cutler took up the post of Australian Ambassador to the Netherlands but had been at The Hague for only a few weeks when he was appointed governor of New South Wales. He was sworn in as governor on 20 January 1966; the Queen had created him a Knight Commander of the Order of St Michael and St George in December 1965.

Cutler retired as governor of New South Wales in 1981. During his distinguished career he had been created a Knight of the Order of St John of Jerusalem in 1965, a Knight Commander of the Royal Victorian Order in 1970, a Companion of the Order of Australia in 1980 and a Knight of the Order of Australia in 1981. He had also received many honorary degrees from universities in New South Wales.

On 28 May 1946 Cutler married Helen Gray Annetta Morris of Bellevue Hill, Sydney, and they have four sons.

Cutler was among the Victoria Cross winners who attended the centenary celebrations in London in 1956. The Australian War Memorial has a portrait of Cutler by Sir William Dargie.

DERRICK Thomas Currie

RANK	Sergeant
UNIT	2/48th Battalion, 26th Brigade, 9th Division
DATE	24 November 1943
PLACE	Sattelberg, New Guinea (now Papua New Guinea)

TOM 'DIVER' DERRICK, born in the Adelaide suburb of Medindie on 20 March 1914 to David and Ada Derrick, was the eldest of a family of two boys and five girls. He was educated at Le Fevre Peninsula school and then learnt carpentry, and was employed for a while at a bakery. In 1931, having lost his job because of the depression, he went to Berri where he made his home until he joined the army in 1940. Initially he got casual work picking fruit but later was working full time on a fruit farm. In May 1939 he married Beryl Violet Leslie.

Derrick enlisted on 5 July 1940 and was allotted to the 2/48th Battalion on 28 August. During the 2/48th's service in Tobruk Derrick was promoted to corporal on 11 July 1941. He was with his unit when it returned to the western desert from Syria and went into action at Tel el Eisa in July 1942. During the fighting around Tel el Eisa Derrick won the Distinguished Conduct Medal on 10 July. In the initial attack he had led an assault on three machine-gun posts and captured many prisoners and in a counter-attack used 'sticky' bombs to damage two tanks.

Derrick's promotion to sergeant was notified on 28 July. On 31 October, during the battle of El Alamein, he was wounded and evacuated. He rejoined his unit in time to return with it to Australia in January 1943.

With the fall of Lae in September 1943 the 7th Division was given the task of clearing the Markham and Ramu Valleys while the 9th Division was to capture Finschhafen, clear the Huon Peninsula, and gain control of the Vitiaz Strait. By 2 October one of the 9th's brigades had occupied Finschhafen but the Japanese were prepared to fight bitterly to retain this strategically important area. On 16–17 October the Japanese launched a sea and land assault and they were only defeated after days of desperate fighting. After the 9th Division was reinforced it switched to the offensive and its 26th Brigade was ordered to capture Sattelberg.

The 2/48th, followed by the 2/23rd, on 22 November reached the southern slopes of Sattelberg about 600 metres from the summit. Fierce resistance was met both here and on the left flank where the 2/23rd Battalion, advancing across very rugged country, began to encircle the enemy position. On the road a landslide prevented further use of tanks and the final assault was left to the infantry. On the 24th a company was ordered to outflank a strong enemy position sited on a precipitous cliff face and then to attack a feature 150 metres from Sattelberg. The only possible approach to the town lay through an open kunai patch situated directly beneath the top of the cliffs and for the next two hours many attempts were made by the Australians to clamber up the slopes to their objective. Each attempt was, however, thwarted by the intense machine-gun fire and grenade bombardment from the Japanese above.

Just before last light the company was ordered to retire, but Derrick requested more time in which to make an assault on the objective. Permission was granted. Derrick moved ahead of his forward section and personally grenaded a post which had halted the company's advance. He ordered his second section around on the right flank and it came under heavy fire from six enemy posts. He again went forward well ahead of the leading men of the section and threw grenade after grenade at the weapon pits above him. The demoralized enemy fled their positions, leaving weapons and grenades, and Derrick's company was able to gain its first foothold on the precipitous ground.

Derrick then returned to the first section and, together with the third section of his platoon, advanced to

144

deal with the three posts which remained in the vicinity. Four times he dashed forward and threw grenades at a range of six to eight metres. Finally the positions were silenced. In all, he had contributed to the silencing of ten enemy posts and, from the vital ground his platoon had captured, the 2/48th moved on to take Sattelberg unopposed the following morning. At 10 a.m. the Australian flag, hoisted by Derrick, was flying over Sattelberg. For his leadership and personal gallantry Derrick was awarded the Victoria Cross.

He was next posted to an officer cadet training unit, graduated lieutenant on 26 November 1944, and rejoined the 2/48th as a reinforcement officer. In May 1945 the 2/48th landed at Tarakan Island and on 22 May was held up at a heavily defended feature named 'Freda' which consisted of several knolls connected by a low saddle. In the fight that ensued two of the knolls were secured by dark, but the enemy launched a fierce counter-attack in the early hours of 23 May. Derrick's platoon on Knoll 2 was in the thick of this action. He was hit in the stomach and thigh but continued to direct operations until evacuated to hospital some hours later. Derrick died next day and was buried in the Tarakan war cemetery. His widow remarried.

Derrick's portrait by Ivor Hele is in the collection of the Australian War Memorial. In 1982 Murray Farquhar, an original member of the 2/48th, wrote a full length biography entitled *Derrick V.C.* His Victoria Cross is now on display in the Hall of Valour at the Australian War Memorial.

EDMONDSON John Hurst

RANK   Corporal
UNIT   2/17th Battalion, 20th Brigade, 9th Division
DATE   13 April 1941
PLACE   Tobruk, Libya

JOHN HURST EDMONDSON was born at Wagga Wagga, New South Wales, on 8 October 1914, the son of Joseph William and Maude Elizabeth Edmondson. As a child he moved with his parents to Liverpool where they took up a farming property. He was educated locally and worked on the farm prior to enlisting in the 2/17th Battalion on 20 May 1940. His militia service with the 4th Battalion (the Australia Rifles) had commenced early in 1939 and many members of that unit formed the nucleus of the 2/17th; Edmondson was thus quickly promoted to corporal on 28 May 1940. After training at Ingleburn and Bathurst the battalion embarked for the Middle East on 19 October.

After brief periods in Palestine, and at Port Said and Mersa Matruh, his unit, as part of the 9th Division, relieved the 6th Australian Division at Marsa Brega in Cyrenaica on 9 March. The new German commander, General Erwin Rommel, seeing how poor the defences were, attacked on 31 March pushing the British forces, including the 20th Brigade, back. The 9th Division stopped at Tobruk where the famous siege began on Good Friday, 11 April 1941.

On the 13th Rommel had most of the *5th Light* and part of the Italian *Ariete Armoured Division* outside Tobruk and he planned to attack early next morning, using a tank regiment and a machine-gun battalion, just west of El Adem road in the 2/17th Battalion's sector. Preceding the attack, the Germans attempted to neutralize Post R33 at 11 p.m. on 13 April when thirty Germans established themselves inside the wire with two guns, a mortar and eight machine-guns. The platoon commander of Post R33, Lieutenant F.A. Mackell, decided to dislodge the enemy with a bayonet charge and he and Edmondson and five privates attacked.

During this counter-attack Edmondson was wounded in the neck and stomach, but he advanced and killed one enemy with his bayonet. Later Mackell was bayoneting a German who held on to him as another came up from behind. Edmondson, some metres away, immediately came to his assistance and in spite of his wounds killed both enemy. The party then returned to Post R33 with a prisoner. Edmondson, badly wounded, died next morning. About 2.30 a.m. 200 Germans again attacked and established a bridgehead in the perimeter. The defence of Post R33 by a handful of men had succeeded in disrupting the German plans by drawing men away from the main attack. By 7.30 a.m. German tanks that had broken through the perimeter were in full retreat. For his conspicuous bravery Edmondson was awarded the Victoria Cross, the first to an Australian in the 1939–45 war. He was buried in the Tobruk war cemetery.

Edmondson's Victoria Cross was presented to his mother by the Governor-General on 27 September 1941. In 1960, watched by Lieutenant Mackell, she presented her son's medals and some of his personal belongings to the Australian War Memorial where they are displayed, near a posthumous portrait by Joshua Smith, in the Hall of Valour. One of the enemy machine-guns captured by the small party from Post R33 is also displayed.

In Liverpool Edmondson's name is commemorated by a clock which stands in the main business section of the town. It was unveiled by the Governor of New South Wales, Lieutenant General Sir John Northcott, in 1957. The Liverpool sub-branch of the Returned Services League has also commemorated him in their Memorial Club House.

EDWARDS Hughie Idwal

RANK   Acting Wing Commander

UNIT   No. 105 Squadron, 2 Group, Bomber Command, RAF

DATE   4 July 1941

PLACE Raid on Bremen, Germany

HUGHIE EDWARDS was born at Fremantle, Western Australia, on 1 August 1914. He was educated at White Gum Valley school near Fremantle and the Fremantle Boys' School. After leaving school he became a shipping office clerk and in early 1934 joined the Garrison Artillery as a private. The following year he was selected for transfer to the RAAF and, upon completion of his training at Point Cook, was transferred to the RAF as a pilot officer.

Edwards was commissioned in the RAF on 21 August 1936 and posted to No. 15 Bomber Squadron. In March 1937 he was appointed adjutant of No. 90 Squadron, flying Blenheims. In August 1938 he was piloting a Blenheim near the Scottish border when he flew into a storm at 2300 metres. When the ailerons froze and the aircraft was forced down to 1600 metres Edwards ordered the crew out. He stayed with the plane, fighting to regain control, but at 230 metres he made an effort to jump clear. His parachute became entangled with the plane's radio mast pylon and in the ensuing crash he sustained head injuries and a badly broken leg. His leg was saved after extensive surgery and Edwards was declared unfit for flying until April 1940 when he joined No. 139 Squadron, which also used Blenheims.

In May 1941 he was appointed to command No. 105 Squadron. At that time his squadron was engaged in a campaign of daylight operations against Germany and the occupied countries; principal targets were enemy shipping north of Dover Strait, power installations, shipbuilding yards, locomotives, steelworks and marshalling yards. On 15 June Edwards led six Blenheims on a search for enemy shipping and sighted a convoy of eight merchantmen at anchor near The Hague. He led the other aircraft in a daring low level attack and his aircraft was responsible for severely damaging, if not sinking, one ship of 4000 tonnes.

Edwards was awarded the Distinguished Flying Cross.

Later, on 4 July, flying Blenheim V6028, Edwards led an important daylight attack on the port of Bremen, one of the most heavily defended towns in Germany. During the approach to the German coast several enemy ships were passed. Edwards knew that his aircraft would be reported and that the Bremen defences would be in a state of readiness. Undaunted, he brought his force of twelve Blenheims eighty kilometres overland at an extremely low level of about fifteen metres, towards the target. When his aircraft reached Bremen they were met with a hail of fire. All were hit, four of them being destroyed. After a successful attack which involved flying under high-tension cables and passing through a balloon barrage, Edwards extricated the surviving aircraft without further loss. For his planning, gallantry and determination, he was awarded the Victoria Cross.

Not long after this exploit, on 28 July 1941, Edwards took No. 105 Squadron to Malta to operate against Axis shipping carrying reinforcements from Italy to Tripoli and Benghazi. They remained until October when the squadron returned to Britain. After participating in a RAF goodwill mission to the United States he was appointed chief flying instructor at an operational training unit in January 1942. On 3 August he again took over No. 105 Squadron, now equipped with Mosquitoes, and led it on more low-level day bombing. In December 1942 on one such raid on the immense Philips radio factory at Eindhoven, the Netherlands, Edwards led a force of ninety-four bombers, thirteen of which were lost. This key installation, however, was heavily damaged and for his leadership Edwards was awarded the Distinguished Service Order, thus making him the first airman to gain the combination of Victoria Cross, DSO and DFC in the 1939–45 war.

In February 1943 he left No. 105 Squadron and became Commanding Officer at the bomber base, Binbrook, where No. 460 Squadron, RAAF, was based, flying Lancasters. Late in December 1944 Edwards went to Ceylon as Group Captain, Bomber Operations, and in January 1945 he became senior administrative staff officer at Headquarters, South-East Asia Command. From November 1945 until February 1946 Edwards was a staff officer at Air Headquarters, Malaya, and after a short period with the Netherlands East Indies Forces returned to Malaya as air adviser to the General Officer Commanding. He next assumed command of RAF Station, Kuala Lumpur, in September and he remained there until May 1947; for his work in South-East Asia he was awarded the OBE in 1947.

Edwards returned to Britain in June 1947, undertook a six months' course at the Staff College, and spent the next two years as senior personnel staff officer of No. 21 Group, Flying Training Command. He was next appointed senior instructor on the leadership course at Digby, Lincolnshire, and after this became station commander at Wattisham, Suffolk.

During the Suez crisis Edwards commanded the RAF Station at Habbaniyah in Iraq and from there he returned to Britain to command, from 21 October 1958, the Central Fighter Establishment, West Raynham, with the rank of air commodore. His last RAF appointment was as Director of Establishments of the Air Ministry, London, a position he held from January 1962 until his retirement on 30 September 1963.

In 1959 Edwards was created a Companion of the Order of the Bath and in March 1960 it was announced that he had been appointed an aide-de-camp to the Queen. He was appointed governor of Western Australia in 1974 and shortly after created KCMG. Also in 1974 he was made a Knight of the Order of St John. He resigned from his vice-regal appointment on 2 April 1975 because of ill health.

Edwards had married Cherry Kyrle in 1942 and they had one son and a daughter. She died in 1966 and Edwards married Dorothy Carew Berrick in 1972. Edwards died in Sydney on 5 August 1982 and his wife donated his orders, decorations and medals to the Australian War Memorial in November 1982 at a ceremony attended by many members of No. 460 Squadron. The Memorial also has a portrait of him by Stella Bowen.

FRENCH John Alexander

RANK   Corporal
UNIT   2/9th Battalion, 18th Brigade, 7th Division
DATE   4 September 1942
PLACE Milne Bay, Papua (now Papua New Guinea)

JOHN ALEXANDER FRENCH was born at Crows Nest, near Toowoomba, Queensland, on 15 July 1914, to Albert and Lucy French. Educated at Crows Nest state school and the technical college, Toowoomba, he then entered his father's hairdressing and tobacconist business. French enlisted on 22 October 1939 and was posted to the 2/9th Battalion, then forming at Redbank, Queensland. He embarked on 5 April 1940 and disembarked in Scotland on 17 June. After training in England and Egypt the 2/9th moved up for action in Libya and took part in the operations at Giarabub, the siege of Tobruk and the garrisoning of Syria. In March 1942 the 2/9th returned to Australia where it remained until August when it embarked for Milne Bay.

On 25–26 August, 2000 Japanese landed in the Milne Bay area and were repulsed by two Australian brigades with RAAF support. By the end of the month the Australians, in search of the Japanese, moved into the K.B. Mission area on the northwestern shore of the bay. The 2/9th moved into the K.B. area on 2 September and, next day, moved along the coast to the east where they encountered the Japanese. After some fighting they pushed on to Sanderson Bay where they went into perimeter defence for the night. Next day, 4 September, French's company crossed a creek about three kilometres from K.B. to attack the Japanese positions at Goroni but ran into terrific machine-gun and rifle fire.

French's own section was held up by three machine-gun posts. After ordering his section to take cover he advanced and silenced the first post with grenades. He then returned for more grenades, advanced again, and silenced the second post. Armed with a Thompson sub-machine gun, he then attacked the third post, firing from the hip as he went forward. French was badly hit from this post and died in front of the gun pit. When his section pushed forward, however, they found that all members of the three enemy gun crews had been killed. By the time the Australian attack was over between sixty and seventy enemy had been killed; a few days later all Japanese resistance had collapsed.

French was buried in the Milne Bay war cemetery. He was unmarried. On 18 July 1958 the Governor-General, Sir William Slim, opened and dedicated the French Memorial Library at Crows Nest which was erected with the aid of funds raised locally.

French's mother visited London in 1956 for the Victoria Cross centenary celebrations.

GORDON James Heather

RANK   Private
UNIT   2/31st Battalion, 25th Brigade, 7th Division
DATE   10 July 1941
PLACE   Near Jezzine (Djezzine), Lebanon

'JIMMY' GORDON was born at Rockingham, Western Australia, on 7 March 1909, son of William Beattie Gordon. When he finished his schooling he worked on his parents' property at Gin Gin, near Perth. He enlisted in the AIF on 26 April 1940 and on 22 September was posted as a reinforcement to the 2/11th Battalion. On the same day he embarked for Palestine where he arrived on 13 October. On 27 February 1941 he was reposted to the 2/31st Battalion.

The Syrian campaign against the Vichy French began on 8 June 1941 with the 2/31st attacking in the centre of three lines of advance. The battalion was about ten kilometres north of Jezzine when news of a possible armistice was received. Before the firing ceased Gordon's company was ordered to capture a feature called 'Greenhill' which overlooked the villages of Amatour and Badarane. About 2.30 a.m. on 10 July, on the right of the attack, the company was held up by intense machine-gun fire and movement, even by single individuals, became very difficult. One officer and two men were killed and others were wounded. The enemy machine-gun position was reinforced and had complete coverage of the area. Gordon, on his own initiative, then crawled out from his position towards the gun. A continuous stream of bullets passed over him and as he got closer the enemy threw grenades which burst above his head. This did not stop Gordon, who leapt to his feet and charged the post. He killed four machine-gunners with his bayonet and his action demoralized other defenders in the area. The main attack then proceeded and the company took the position. They were then ordered to withdraw from the new positions at 5 a.m. After all the enemy arms and equipment had been destroyed, the company fought its way back to the battalion. Gordon further distinguished himself in these subsequent actions.

In March 1942 his unit returned to Australia and served in the campaign in the Owen Stanleys in Papua. In September 1943 the 2/31st participated in the capture of Lae and subsequent operations in the Markham and Ramu Valleys. Its final campaign at Balikpapan, Borneo, commenced on 1 July 1945. Gordon had been promoted to corporal on 26 September 1941 and to sergeant on 28 January 1943.

Gordon returned to farming after his demobilization, but in December 1947 re-enlisted in the newly formed Australian regular army and was posted to the 30th Cadet Battalion at Karrakatta, Western Australia. Later he was posted to the 5th Cadet Brigade Training Depot in Fremantle and rose to the rank of warrant officer class II. He retired from the army on 1 August 1968 and then worked as a groundsman at Campbell Barracks, Swanbourne, Western Australia, until 1975.

Gordon had married Myrtle Anzac Troy in 1940 and they had one son. He still lives in Western Australia. A portrait of him by Sir William Dargie hangs in the Australian War Memorial's Hall of Valour.

GRATWICK Percival Eric

RANK	Private
UNIT	2/48th Battalion, 26th Brigade, 9th Division
DATE	25–26 October 1942
PLACE	Battle of El Alamein, Egypt

PERCY GRATWICK was born at Katanning, Western Australia, on 19 October 1902, to Ernest Albert and Eva Mary Gratwick. Before his enlistment in the AIF, on 20 December 1940, he was working as a gold prospector. He embarked on 5 July 1941, was posted to the 2/48th Battalion and joined this unit on 17 September in besieged Tobruk. When relieved in Tobruk the 2/48th went as part of the Syria garrison but returned to North Africa in July 1942 to participate in the fighting around Tel el Eisa. The battle of El Alamein opened on 23 October with the 2/48th attacking on the flank of the British attack.

The battle had been in progress for about forty-eight hours when the 2/48th was ordered to capture the point known as Trig 29 on Miteiriya (or 'Ruin') Ridge which was considered tactically vital as it commanded the area of attack. The 2/48th advanced at midnight on 25 October supported by a specially formed mobile company of machine-gun carriers. After fierce hand-to-hand fighting the position was captured.

The actions for which Gratwick was awarded the Victoria Cross came early in the attack when his company, advancing on the left flank, was forced to ground by well-directed fire from the elevated enemy positions. The platoon commander, platoon sergeant and many others in Gratwick's platoon were killed, the total strength being reduced to seven. Gratwick then quickly got up and charged the nearest enemy post with a rifle and bayonet in one hand, and a grenade in the other. Throwing one grenade into the post, then another, he jumped in among the surviving defenders with his bayonet and killed them all, including a complete mortar crew. He then charged through heavy machine-gun fire towards a second post, and inflicted further casualties. Gratwick was killed by a burst of machine-gun fire just short of the enemy trench. The enemy were unnerved, however, and Gratwick's company was able to move forward and capture its objective.

Gratwick was buried in the Tel el Eisa cemetery on 27 October 1942, but was later reinterred in the El

Alamein military cemetery. In October 1956 a clubroom known as the Gratwick Soldiers' Club was opened at Campbell Barracks, Swanbourne, Western Australia. In July 1957 his relatives presented his medals to the club where they are displayed in a cabinet constructed of West Australian jarrah.

GURNEY Arthur Stanley

RANK	Private
UNIT	2/48th Battalion, 26th Brigade, 9th Division
DATE	22 July 1942
PLACE	Tel el Eisa, Egypt

A.S. GURNEY was born at Dayawn, Western Australia, on 15 December 1908, son of George Gurney. The family, including two boys and three girls, later settled in the Perth suburb of Victoria Park. Stan Gurney was employed by the Perth Electric-

ity and Gas Depot and was a skilled professional cyclist.

He enlisted on 6 December 1940 and embarked at Fremantle for the Middle East on 6 July 1941. Gurney was then posted to the 2/48th Battalion on 12 September when that unit was part of the Tobruk garrison. After Tobruk Gurney accompanied his unit to Syria where it was employed on garrison duties before it returned to Egypt.

Units of the 9th Australian Division were heavily committed to the fighting at Tel el Eisa in July 1942 in what was a prelude to the decisive battle of El Alamein. By the end of June 1942 Rommel's forces in their offensive had reached El Alamein and threatened to overrun Egypt. The weakened Eighth British Army was holding a defensive line only 115 kilometres from the main base at Alexandria. Australian troops were moved from Syria late in June and by the end of July the 9th Division had been in four actions. These actions were sharp and bitter, especially around the small railway station at Tel el Eisa and a nearby feature which rose twenty-five metres from the desert. Both sides lost heavily but the British stabilized their line and the initiative had been seized from the enemy. The British were then able to build up strength for the decisive battles of October.

Gurney won his Victoria Cross during an attack at Tel el Eisa on 22 July. His company was held up by intense machine-gun fire from posts 100 metres in front, and all the officers were killed or wounded. Gurney, without hesitation, charged the nearest machine-gun post, bayoneted three men and silenced the post. He continued on to the second post, bayoneted two men and sent a third out as prisoner. Stick grenades were thrown at him and he was knocked to the ground, but he got up and charged the third post. Gurney disappeared from view and later his body was found in an enemy post. His brave bayonet charge had, however, enabled his company to advance to its objective and inflict heavy casualties on the enemy.

Gurney was buried in the war cemetery at El Alamein. His Victoria Cross, the first of four awarded to members of the 2/48th Battalion (*see* Kibby, Gratwick and Derrick), was presented to the Perth Returned Services League by his family. On 2 August 1957 the Australian Army Canteens Service opened a new soldiers' club at Karrakatta camp, called the Gurney Club.

KELLIHER Richard

RANK   Private
UNIT   2/25th Battalion, 25th
          Brigade, 7th Division
DATE   13 September 1943
PLACE   Near Nadzab, New
          Guinea (now Papua
          New Guinea)

RICHARD KELLIHER was born on 1 September 1910 at Ballybeggan, Tralee, County Kerry, Ireland. He migrated from Ireland and was working in Brisbane, Queensland, as a labourer when he enlisted in the AIF on 21 February 1941. He was reposted to the 2/12th Battalion on 26 June and the following day embarked to join his unit in the Middle East. On 11 October he was posted to the 2/25th Battalion and joined the unit when it was performing garrison duties in Syria after the campaign. The unit returned to Australia in March 1942 then moved to New Guinea and participated in the fighting in the Owen Stanleys and at

Gona. After re-equipping in Australia it next fought in the operations at Nadzab and Lae which began in September 1943.

In early September the 7th and 9th Divisions advanced on Lae from different directions. On the 7th Division front leading elements of the 2/25th had progressed over one-third of the distance to Lae when the first serious opposition developed, on 10 September, at Jensen's plantation.

The Japanese resisted for a time but the 2/25th advanced through and, by 12 September, had reached Whittaker's plantation. They then encountered well-constructed positions defended by Japanese marines who resisted stubbornly. The pressure was increased and by nightfall on the 13th two companies of the 2/25th were positioned on high ground overlooking the next objective, Heath's plantation, which was taken the following day.

It was during the advance between Whittaker's and Heath's that Kelliher performed the deeds for which he was awarded the Victoria Cross. On the morning of the 13th his platoon came under heavy fire from a concealed machine-gun post fifty metres away. Five of the platoon were killed and three wounded including his section commander, Corporal W.H. Richards. Kelliher said to a companion, 'I'd better go and bring him [Richards] in', then suddenly got up, rushed the post and hurled two grenades at it. When he ascertained that some, but not all, of the enemy had been killed he returned to his section, seized a Bren gun, and again dashed forward to

within thirty metres of the post and with accurate fire completely silenced it. He then went forward again, through heavy rifle fire, and successfully rescued his section leader who had been wounded in the shoulder.

Kelliher next fought in the Markham and Ramu Valleys and at Balikpapan in Borneo. In 1946 he went to London as a member of the Australian contingent for the Victory parade; ten years later he attended the Victoria Cross centenary celebrations.

After the war Kelliher lived in Burwood, a suburb of Melbourne, Victoria, and was employed at the Burnley Horticultural School. On 30 August 1949 he married Olive Margaret Hearn and they had a family of two daughters and a son. On 16 January 1963 he suffered a stroke and died twelve days later at Heidelberg Repatriation Hospital. He was buried at Springvale cemetery. His widow remarried.

In 1965 his widow put his medals up for auction in London but withdrew them after sharp reaction from ex-servicemen. An appeal was launched by the 2/25th Battalion Association who raised sufficient funds to buy the medals which they presented to the Australian War Memorial on 13 September 1966 for inclusion in Victoria Cross Corner; Kelliher's VC is now displayed in the Hall of Valour. The Australian War Memorial also has a portrait of him by George Browning.

KENNA Edward

RANK	Private
UNIT	2/4th Battalion, 19th Brigade, 6th Division
DATE	15 May 1945
PLACE	Near Wewak, New Guinea (now Papua New Guinea)

TED KENNA was born at Hamilton, Victoria, on 6 July 1919, son of Bryan F. Kenna. He was educated at St Mary's Convent, Hamilton, and worked as a plumber after leaving school. Kenna was a keen cyclist and footballer and served in the Citizen Military Forces. He enlisted in the AIF on 9 August 1940 and, after service in the 23rd/21st Battalion, was posted to the 2/4th Battalion on 3 September 1943. His unit embarked at Cairns for New Guinea on 28 October 1944.

In early May 1945 the 6th Division was near the end of its 130 kilometre advance from Aitape and on 10–11 May the port and former air base of Wewak was captured by the 2/4th Battalion. The Japanese who escaped from Wewak made for their next line of defence which was situated in rugged terrain to the south. From Wirui Mission in this sector the enemy had shelled the Australians and it became necessary for the 2/4th to climb into the hills to eliminate the threat.

On 14 May the 2/4th Battalion, supported by tanks, attacked Wirui Mission from the east and after a sharp fight took all but the north-western spur. Three posts remained and the next day these were attacked by a platoon of the 2/4th. Two sections attacked but were halted by intense fire after several men were hit. Kenna, in the support section, endeavoured to bring his gun to bear on the bunker, but was unable to because of the nature of the ground. Without orders, and on his own initiative, he immediately stood up in full view of the Japanese and engaged the bunker with a Bren gun, then a rifle and then a Bren gun again. The enemy machine-gunners were only fifty metres away from him and their fire was so accurate that bullets passed between his arms and body but miraculously did not hit him. The remaining post was then knocked out by a tank and the attack was successfully concluded; many enemy were killed and several automatic weapons were captured. For his coolness and bravery Kenna was awarded the Victoria Cross.

Three weeks later, on 5 June 1945, in similar operations further inland, he was struck in the mouth by an explosive bullet and subsequently hospitalized. He was discharged in December 1946 and on 6 January 1947, at Government House, Melbourne, the Duke of Gloucester presented him with his Victoria Cross. On 2 June 1947 he married Marjorie Ellen Rushberry, who had nursed him at Heidelberg Military Hospital; they have two sons and two daughters.

Kenna returned to Hamilton, worked for a period at the Borough Hall, then became curator of the Melville Oval. He went to London to attend the coronation in 1953 and for several Victoria Cross reunions including the 1956 Victoria Cross centenary celebrations. He still lives at Hamilton.

KIBBY William Henry

RANK	Sergeant
UNIT	2/48th Battalion, 26th Brigade, 9th Division
DATE	23–31 October 1942
PLACE	Battle of El Alamein, Egypt

WILLIAM KIBBY was born at Winlaton, Durham, UK, on 15 April 1903 to John Robert and Mary Isabella Kibby. With his parents he migrated to Australia in 1914 and settled at Glenelg, South Australia. He was employed as a fibrous plaster fixer and interior decorator when he enlisted in the AIF on 29 June 1940. Kibby was posted to the 2/48th Battalion on 27 August and soon after, on 14 September, was promoted to corporal; a month later he was promoted to sergeant.

He embarked with his unit at Adelaide on 17 November and after training in Palestine the 26th Brigade moved to Derna. After the German breakthrough on 31 March 1941 Kibby's brigade moved back to Tobruk where, with the rest of the 9th Australian Division, it held Tobruk from April to October 1941. Following its relief the battalion performed garrison duties in Syria until its return to Egypt in June 1942. Kibby broke his leg shortly after arriving in the Middle East and was medically downgraded. He faced the prospect of being transferred to a training battalion but just before the action at Tel el Eisa in July 1942 he succeeded in having himself included in some reinforcements for the 2/48th.

On the night of the commencement of the battle of El Alamein, 23 October 1942, the 2/48th was the right-hand battalion on the Eighth Army's front. During the initial attack at Miteiriya Ridge, on the 23rd, Kibby's platoon commander was killed. No sooner had Kibby assumed command than his platoon was ordered to attack an enemy machine-gun post. He got up, called his platoon forward, and charged the post firing his Tommy gun. His platoon did not hear his command because of the battle noise, so Kibby single-handedly silenced the post, killing three of the enemy and capturing twelve others. His company then continued the advance.

After the capture of Trig 29 on 26 October intense enemy bombardments and tank and infantry counter-attacks were directed against the Australians. Throughout this period Kibby moved from section to section directing the fire of his men. Several times, under intense machine-gun fire, he went out and mended the platoon line communi-cations which enabled mortar concentrations to be still effectively directed against the attack on his company's front.

Kibby distinguished himself again on the night of 30–31 October when the 2/48th attacked 'ring contour' 25. Kibby's platoon had to move through withering machine-gun fire to reach its objective. Kibby went out alone to knock out the last enemy post which hindered the 2/48th's advance. Although he destroyed the enemy post with grenades, he was himself killed by a burst of machine-gun fire. The 2/48th captured its final objective soon after.

A note was found in the pocket of Kibby's dead company commander (Captain Peter Robbins) which recommended Kibby for the 'highest possible decoration' for his actions on the 23rd. For that action and the subsequent ones Kibby was posthumously awarded the Victoria Cross. He was buried in the war cemetery at El Alamein. His widow attended the Victoria Cross centenary celebrations in London in 1956. A house at Helmsdale, South Australia, was purchased by a memorial trust for the use of his family.

KINGSBURY Bruce Steel

RANK	Private
UNIT	2/14th Battalion, 21st Brigade, 7th Division
DATE	29 August 1942
PLACE	Isurava (Kokoda trail), Papua (now Papua New Guinea)

BRUCE KINGSBURY was born at Armadale, Melbourne, on 8 January 1918 to Philip Blencowe and Florence Annie Kingsbury. He was educated at the Hawksburn state school and won a scholarship to the Melbourne Technical College. He then entered the real estate business in Melbourne and subsequently farmed in the Mallee district of Victoria. He became a station hand at Boundary Bend, moved to various jobs in New South Wales, and returned to Victoria to enter his father's real estate business in Northcote.

Kingsbury enlisted in the AIF on 29 May 1940 and was posted to the 2/2nd Pioneer Battalion, but on 7 June joined the 2/14th Battalion. Kingsbury embarked with his unit on 19 October and served in Egypt and Syria. In January 1942 he returned to Palestine and then to Australia where he disembarked in March. In August his unit was moved to Port Moresby and by late August met the Japanese on the Kokoda Trail.

The action for which Kingsbury was awarded the Victoria Cross took place in the first major campaign in Papua when the Japanese pushed a force southward from Buna and Gona across the Owen Stanleys towards Port Moresby. From 27 August the 2/14th had been holding positions on the main line of the Japanese advance at Isurava about 13 kilometres past Kokoda on the trail over the mountains. The Japanese attacked incessantly and on the 29th increased their pressure. Kingsbury was one of a party from headquarters company and the signal platoon sent up to assist the defenders in the forward positions. When the enemy broke through on the right flank and threatened battalion headquarters Kingsbury, whose own platoon was decimated by the enemy, joined a different platoon which was to counter-attack. He rushed forward, firing his Bren gun and cleared a path through the enemy while at the same time causing a high number of casualties. He was shot dead by a sniper but not before he had saved battalion headquarters and contributed to the position being held.

He was buried at the Kokoda war

cemetery. Kingsbury was unmarried. His Victoria Cross, the first gained on territory administered by Australia and the first awarded in the South-West Pacific Area, is in a Melbourne collection.

MACKEY John Bernard

RANK   Corporal
UNIT   2/3rd Pioneer
          Battalion,
          9th Division
DATE   12 May 1945
PLACE Tarakan Island, East
          Indies (now Indonesia)

JOHN MACKEY was born on 16 May 1922 at Leichhardt, Sydney, to Stanley and Bridget Catherine Mackey. Educated at St Columba's School and the Christian Brothers high school, Lewisham, Mackey was a keen rugby league player. At the time of his enlistment in the AIF he was working in his father's bakery at Portland, New South Wales.

He was posted to the 2/3rd Pioneer Battalion on 22 February 1941, embarked at Sydney on 1 November and served with his unit in the Middle East until its return to Australia in February 1943 after the battle of El Alamein. In August 1943 the 2/3rd embarked for New Guinea. During operations at Finschhafen, on 26 October, Mackey was promoted to corporal. The 2/3rd Pioneers returned to Australia in March 1944 but by May 1945 were back in action at Tarakan.

Tarakan Island before the war was an important oilfield, but the Allies' principal reason for attacking it on 1 May 1945 was to secure an airfield for pending operations against the Borneo mainland. The 2/3rd Pioneers, in the south-western section, came under heavy fire on 7 May and were held up but by the 9th they had forced the enemy back to 'Helen', a strongly fortified feature east of Tarakan town. The forward companies, which had been in action for three successive days, were relieved and on the 12th one of the fresh companies attacked after heavy artillery and mortar fire. Mackey's section was moving along a narrow spur with scarcely width for more than one man when it came under fire from three well-sited positions near the top of a very steep, razor-backed ridge. Mackey charged the first light machine-gun post, overcame it in a hand-to-hand struggle, then turned on a heavy machine-gun post and killed the crew by throwing a grenade through the firing slit of their bunker. He changed his rifle for an

Owen gun and charged up a steep slope towards another light machine-gun position. He was within a few metres of the post when he was killed by machine-gun fire but not before he had killed two more enemy. His platoon then fought its way on to its objective from where the company was able to engage the enemy. The Japanese, however, stood firm until the 14th when napalm was dropped from aircraft and drove them from 'Helen'.

For his outstanding courage Mackey was awarded the Victoria Cross. He was buried in Labuan war cemetery and in 1946 his Victoria Cross was presented to his sister, Patricia Mackey, at Admiralty House, Sydney, by the Governor-General, the Duke of Gloucester. His sister donated it to the Australian War Memorial and it is now displayed in the Hall of Valour. Mackey's name is commemorated by an individual plaque on the front of the Leichhardt War Memorial in Pioneers Park, Leichhardt.

MIDDLETON Rawdon Hume

RANK	Flight Sergeant
UNIT	RAAF, attached to No. 149 Squadron, 3 Group, Bomber Command, RAF
DATE	28–29 November 1942
PLACE	Raid on Turin, Italy

R.H. MIDDLETON was born at Waverley, New South Wales, on 22 July 1916, to Francis Rawdon and Faith Lillian Middleton. He moved with his parents to Yarrabandai, New South Wales, where his father managed Leewang Station. Educated at the Dubbo high school, he was a keen cricketer and footballer and upon leaving worked as a jackeroo on Leewang Station.

On 14 October 1940 he enlisted in the RAAF, training in Australia, Canada and the United Kingdom under the Empire Air Training Scheme. He joined No. 7 Squadron on 1 January 1942 but on 26 February transferred to No. 149 (East India) Squadron to fly Short Stirling heavy bombers. In the next few months he acted as second pilot in raids on the Ruhr and on 31 July, his eleventh operational sortie, captained an aircraft in a raid against Düsseldorf. He was then involved in sorties to Duisburg, Osnabrück, Frankfurt, Wilhelmshaven and Munich, and several minelaying trips. On 7 November he flew in a raid on Genoa and on the 20th the target was the Royal Arsenal, Turin. Eight days later he participated in a raid on the Fiat works at Turin and performed the actions for which he was awarded the Victoria Cross. His commission as a pilot officer, backdated to 14 November 1942, was subsequently gazetted.

On his twenty-ninth sortie he was captain of Stirling BF372, an aircraft he had flown only once before. His gunners had all completed their tour of thirty operations but volunteered to stay with Middleton for his last two trips. On the outward journey Middleton experienced difficulty in climbing to the necessary altitude to cross the Alps. Once across he made three low altitude flights over Turin so that the target could be identified. The aircraft was then subjected to fire from light anti-aircraft guns and a shell burst in the cockpit, shattering the windscreen and wounding both pilots. A piece of shell splinter tore into the side of Middleton's face destroying his right eye and exposing the bone over the eye. The second pilot and wireless operator were also wounded. Middleton lost consciousness and the aircraft dived to 250 metres before control was regained by the second pilot who took the plane up to 500 metres and released the bombs.

Middleton recovered consciousness, ordered the second pilot back to receive first aid, and set course for base. After discussing various alternatives Middleton decided to try and make the English coast so that his crew could leave the aircraft by parachute. He knew that he had little chance of saving himself. Four hours later, after an Alpine crossing, the French coast was reached and Middleton took evasive action when the aircraft was engaged by light anti-aircraft fire. After the plane had crossed the channel it only had sufficient fuel for five minutes flying. Middleton ordered his crew to abandon the aircraft while he flew parallel with the coast for a few kilometres, after which he intended to head out to sea. Five of the crew left the aircraft safely while two remained to assist him. The aircraft crashed in the sea and the bodies of the front gunner and flight engineer were recovered the following day. Middleton's body was washed ashore at Shakespeare Beach, Dover, on 1 February 1943. He was buried in the churchyard of St John's, Beck Row, Mildenhall, Suffolk, with full military honours.

In May 1949 a painting by David Smith, formerly of No. 149 Squadron, of Middleton's Stirling in its last moments of flight was presented to the Australian War Memorial. A posthumous portrait by Harold Freedman and Middleton's Victoria Cross and other medals and RAAF tunic are displayed in the Australian War Memorial's Hall of Valour. He was unmarried.

The citation for the Victoria Cross ended with the following sentence: 'His devotion to duty in the face of overwhelming odds is unsurpassed in the annals of the Royal Air Force'.

NEWTON William Ellis

RANK   Flight Lieutenant
UNIT   No. 22 Squadron, RAAF
DATE   16 March 1943
PLACE   Salamaua Isthmus, New Guinea (now Papua New Guinea)

'BILL' NEWTON was born on 8 June 1919 at St Kilda, Victoria, to Charles Ellis and Minnie Newton. He was educated at Melbourne Grammar School where he was a sergeant in the Cadet Corps. He was an excellent cricketer. Upon leaving school he was employed at a Melbourne city warehouse. Called up early in 1940 he trained in Australia, was commissioned pilot officer on 28 June 1940 and completed advanced training at Point Cook on 9 September. He was posted as an instructor and promoted to flying officer on 28 December. He continued as an instructor during 1941 and after being promoted to flight lieutenant on 1 April 1942 achieved his ambition of being posted to an operational squadron on 9 May.

He flew fifty-two operational sorties with No. 22 Attack Squadron, which was equipped with Boston bombers. He was awarded the Victoria Cross for his great courage during his ten months' operational flying, but was particularly cited for his actions on 16 March 1943.

These included repeated raids on the isthmus of Salamaua, at that stage a vital enemy coastal base. On three occasions Newton dived his Boston through intense anti-aircraft fire to release bombs on important targets. On one occasion his starboard engine failed over the target, but he succeeded in flying back to an airfield 260 kilometres away.

On 16 March, two days before his last flight, he led an attack through intense and accurate shell fire and, although his aircraft was hit repeatedly, he held to his course and bombed his target from a low level. The attack resulted in the destruction of many buildings and dumps including two 40 000-gallon fuel installations. His aircraft was crippled, with fuselage and wing sections torn, petrol tanks pierced, main-planes and engines seriously damaged, and one of the main tyres flat, but he managed to fly back to base and make a successful landing.

Two days later he returned to the same locality. His target was a single building. He attacked it through a barrage of fire, but as he scored a hit his aircraft burst into flames. He kept the aircraft in the air for as long as he could to get the crew as far away as possible from the enemy's positions. With great skill he brought his blazing aircraft down on the water. Newton and Flight Sergeant J. Lyon were then able to swim away from the wreck. When they got ashore they were captured by troops of *No. 5 Sasebo Special Naval Landing Force.* Both were sent to Lae where Lyon was later executed on the orders of the naval commander for the Lae-Salamaua area, Rear Admiral Fujita. Newton was returned to Salamaua on the orders of Fujita and was executed on 29 March by the Japanese naval sub-lieutenant who had captured him.

Newton's death was closely linked for several years with one of three 'execution photographs' which were published throughout the world. They were, however, of an Australian army sergeant who was executed at Aitape several months after Newton. Newton's executioner was later killed in the Philippines and Fujita committed suicide at the war's end.

In September 1943 the Allies captured the Japanese-held airfield at Nadzab and named the subsequently developed No. 4 strip Newton Field in his honour. There are several other memorials to Newton in Melbourne including an oval at the St Kilda Cricket Club, a plaque at the Victoria Golf Club, and a memorial panel in the St Kilda Presbyterian Church. In May 1952 a posthumous potrait was presented to the RAAF College, Point Cook and another posthumous portrait, by Alfred H. Cook, commissioned by the Commonwealth, hangs in the Australian War Memorial's Hall of Valour.

Newton's body was recovered when Australian troops captured Salamaua six months after his death, and he was buried in the Salamaua war cemetery.

His mother, Mrs Minnie Newton, received his Victoria Cross from the Governor-General, the Duke of Gloucester, at Melbourne on 30 November 1945. She subsequently donated them to the Australian War Memorial where they are now displayed in the Hall of Valour. Although he was the fourth Australian airman to win the Victoria Cross, he was the only member of the RAAF to win the award as a member of an RAAF squadron under RAAF control.

PARTRIDGE Frank John

RANK   Private
UNIT   8th Battalion, 23rd
         Brigade, II Australian
         Corps
DATE   24 July 1945
PLACE Bonis Peninsula,
         Bougainville (now
         Papua New Guinea)

FRANK PARTRIDGE was born at Grafton, New South Wales, on 29 November 1924, the son of Patrick James and Mary Partridge. His father was a dairy farmer and banana grower at Upper Newee Creek, Macksville. Partridge was educated at Tewinga public school, and after leaving school worked on the family property with his two brothers and a sister. Following service in the Volunteer Defence Corps he enlisted in the AIF on 26 March 1943.

Partridge was posted to the 8th Battalion which was part of the 23rd Brigade, an original brigade of the ill-fated 8th Division which had been reconstituted with militia battalions. After jungle warfare training on the Atherton Tableland he embarked for Lae, New Guinea, in May 1944. In September 1944 the 23rd Brigade moved to occupy the outer Solomon Islands. The 8th Battalion moved to Emirau Island, north-west of New Ireland, and by April 1945 elements of it were disposed on Emirau, Green and Treasury Islands. The other two battalions of the brigade had moved to Bougainville and in June, the 8th Battalion joined the 23rd Brigade there, taking part in the last series of actions fought by Australians on that island. Partridge's battalion operated in the northern section with the aim of containing the enemy in the Bonis Peninsula area.

On 23 July the 8th Battalion launched a company attack against a ridge and successfully took it. On the afternoon of the 24th two platoons were given the task of eliminating an enemy post which prevented the 8th's advance. The troops reached the first ridge without difficulty, but then came under fierce machine-gun, grenade and rifle fire. Partridge's section came under particularly heavy fire and he was hit twice, in the left arm and the left thigh. Despite his wounds, and disregarding the heavy fire, he retrieved a Bren gun from a dead gunner and passed it on to another man and told him to give covering fire. He then rushed the enemy bunker, silenced it with a grenade, and killed the only living occupant with his knife. He cleared the dead from the entrance to the bunker and rushed another bunker but loss of blood caused him to halt and call for aid. His platoon moved forward but overwhelming enemy fire caused it to withdraw. The whole position was not taken that day but was abandoned by the Japanese soon after.

On 11 August active patrolling ceased in all sectors of Bougainville. Partridge was awarded the Victoria Cross for his part in the action on the 24th and his award was the first made to a militia man. He received his Victoria Cross from the Governor-General, the Duke of Gloucester, at Sydney on 13 April 1946.

After his discharge from the army he made three journeys to London: in 1946 he was a member of the Australian contingent for the Victory march; in 1953 he attended the coronation; and in 1956 Partridge was present at the Victoria Cross centenary celebrations.

Partridge operated a banana plantation at Upper Newee Creek and was vice-president of the Nambucca District Council of the Banana Growers' Federation. He served on the executive of the local sub-branch of the Returned Services League, and was a life member of the Macksville and District Ex-Servicemen's Club. He was very successful in radio and television quiz programmes and in the 1963 elections was campaign manager for the Country Party in the electorate of Cowper.

On 23 March 1964 Partridge was killed in a car accident near Bellingen, New South Wales, and was buried with full military honours at Macksville. He had married Barbara Dunlop on 23 February 1963 and their son was born in December of that year. A memorial plaque was unveiled in Nambucca Heads Returned Services' League Club, Belligen, by Sir John Northcott, on 31 October 1964.

RATTEY Reginald Roy

RANK	Corporal
UNIT	25th Battalion, 7th Brigade, 3rd Division
DATE	22 March 1945
PLACE	Near Tokinotu, Bougainville (now Papua New Guinea)

REG RATTEY, born at Barmedman, New South Wales, on 28 March 1918, son of Albert J. Rattey, was the eldest of a family of five boys and two girls. Educated at Bellarwi public school, he later worked on the family's 728 hectare property at Bellarwi in the Wyalong district. A keen sportsman, he played cricket, football and tennis.

On 24 September 1941 he entered the army and transferred to the AIF in July 1942. His unit, the 3rd Division (later 11th Division) Carrier Company embarked for New Guinea on 3 September 1943 and, in the next year, served at Port Moresby, Soputa and in the Gusap area. Rattey had, however, returned to Australia in April 1944 and on 9 June was posted to the 25th Battalion (the Darling Downs Regiment); he had been promoted to corporal on 8 February.

His new unit had already served in New Guinea in 1942–43 and it embarked again on 20 July 1944 for the Madang area where it remained until it moved to Bougainville in November for its final actions.

Rattey won his Victoria Cross during a particularly bitter phase of the campaign in south Bougainville as the Australians attempted to force their way down the road to Buin against fierce opposition from elements of the Japanese 6th Division. The 25th crossed the Puriata River on 4 March and met strong opposition. One company was surrounded and repeatedly attacked for three days. Soon a Japanese force of considerable strength was moving about between the forward and rear companies of the 25th. On 19 March the battalion began a thrust down the Buin road on a two-company front with the object of clearing the road as far as Tokinotu where the forward company was deployed. The 25th encountered an extensive system of pillboxes at a road junction, and two platoons made a bayonet charge which dislodged the enemy from part of this stronghold. The Japanese fell back to new positions which were bombarded by aircraft and artillery, on 22 March, prior to the attack by Rattey's company.

Rattey led his section firing a Bren gun from the hip until he was on top of the first Japanese weapon-pit. He flung in a grenade and called his men forward. Using the same tactics he killed the Japanese in two more weapon-pits. He then advanced on a Japanese machine-gun post and with his Bren gun killed one of the team, wounded another, and put the rest to flight. Some 2000 rounds of ammunition were found beside the gun. Rattey's action enabled the advance to continue and the company gained its objective within the hour.

Two days later Rattey was promoted to sergeant. He returned to Australia shortly before the end of the war and toured New South Wales promoting the Australian Comfort Fund's 'Salute to Valour' drive for money. After his discharge from the AIF he returned to his home district and farming. He visited London in 1946 as a member of the victory contingent when he was personally invested by King George VI. He visited London again for the coronation in 1953. He attended the Victoria Cross centenary celebrations in 1956 and some of the subsequent reunions of the Victoria Cross and George Cross Association which are held in London.

Rattey's portrait by J.B. Godson is

in the Australian War Memorial. His first wife, who died, was Emily Joyce Cafe. He married Aileen Delany on 11 January 1955 and their family consists of one boy and three girls.

STARCEVICH Leslie Thomas

RANK   Private
UNIT   2/43rd Battalion, 24th Brigade, 9th Division
DATE   28 June 1945
PLACE Near Beaufort, British North Borneo (now Malaysia)

'STARCEY' STARCEVICH was born at Subiaco, Western Australia, on 5 September 1918. After leaving Richmeadows school, Grass Patch, he worked on his father's farm until he was nineteen. He then became a gold miner at Norseman. He enlisted in the AIF on 9 April 1941, embarked at Fremantle on 9 September and joined the 2/43rd on 30 December in Palestine. His unit was posted to Syria for garrison duty in January 1942 and remained there until June before returning to the Western Desert. The 2/43rd fought at Tel el Eisa where Starcevich was wounded on 17 July. He rejoined the battalion in time to take part in the battle of El Alamein.

The unit returned to Australia in February 1943 and left in September for New Guinea, where it joined in the fighting at Lae and Finschhafen. Early in 1944 it returned to Australia but in April 1945 was allotted to the Borneo campaign.

It was during the 9th Division's campaign in British North Borneo, which began on 10 June, that Starcevich was awarded the Victoria Cross. After the capture of Labuan Island, mainland landings were made on the northern reaches of Brunei Bay and a two-pronged drive on Beaufort was commenced.

The 2/43rd attacked Beaufort on the afternoon of the 27th and by dusk one company had advanced into the town itself. The Japanese counter-attacked during the night and isolated the company in Beaufort. B Company, of which Starcevich was a member, was ordered forward to the beleaguered company's aid. As the Australians moved down a single track, which followed a wooded spur, towards the enemy positions they came under fire from two enemy machine-gun posts and suffered casualties. Starcevich, a Bren-gunner, walked forward firing from the hip. He assaulted each post in turn, killing five enemy and putting the rest to flight. The advance progressed until the section came under fire from another machine-gun post. Starcevich, without regard for his own safety, rushed the post and captured it after killing seven enemy. By 29 June the fight was virtually over and that day was spent mopping up the remaining Japanese force.

After the war the civilian population of Beaufort erected a tablet near the spot where the action occurred and named the jungle track Victoria Cross Road. Starcevich was decorated by Sir James Mitchell, the Governor of Western Australia, on 28 August 1947 and the following December married Kathleen B. Hardy. They had two sons and a daughter. He attended the Victoria Cross centenary celebrations in London in 1956 and served in the Citizen Forces in the 11th/44th Battalion. He spent four years after the war as a car salesman before taking up sheep and wheat farming at Carnamah, Western Australia. He later moved to Norseman, then to Grass Patch where he still lives. The Australian War Memorial has in its collection a portrait of him by George Browning.

Vietnam 1962–72

BADCOE Peter John

RANK	Major
UNIT	Australian Army Training Team, Vietnam
DATE	23 February – 7 April 1967
PLACE	Phu Tho, Quang Dien and Huong Tra districts, Thua Thien province, South Vietnam (now the Socialist Republic of Vietnam)

PETER BADCOE was born in Adelaide on 11 January 1934 and was educated in his home city. He joined the South Australian public service as a clerk. Early in 1952 he served for seven weeks in the 16th National Service Battalion and on 12 July entered the Officer Cadet School, Portsea, Victoria, from which he graduated second lieutenant on 13 December 1952.

Early postings included the 14th National Service Training Battalion and 1st Field Regiment, Royal Australian Artillery. From late 1958 until 1961 he served in the Directorate of Military Operations and Plans at Army Headquarters as a general staff officer grade III. He returned to regimental duties with the 4th Field Regiment on 6 February 1961 and in June of that year was posted to the 103rd Field Battery, with whom he served a tour of duty in Malaya as a battery captain. After a third period with the 1st Field Regiment, November 1963 to August 1965, Badcoe changed his corps from artillery to infantry. He was promoted to temporary major on 10 August 1965 and posted to the Infantry Centre at Ingleburn, New South Wales.

In August 1966 Badcoe realized his ambition to serve in Vietnam when he was posted to the Australian Army Training Team there as sub-sector adviser to the Nam Hoa district of Thua Thien province. As an adviser he was concerned with military operations and training carried out by the Ruff Puffs in his district.

In December he was reallotted to the sector headquarters of Thua Thien as operations adviser. Normally he would have been responsible for planning, liaison and associated staff work, but he took full advantage of the latitude given to advisers to lead forces into action whenever the opportunity arose. It was as province (or sector) operations adviser that he carried out the following actions for which he was awarded the Victoria Cross.

On 23 February 1967 he was acting as adviser to a regional force company in support of a sector operation in Phu Tho district when he monitored a radio transmission which reported the death of an American subsector adviser and the wounding of an American medical adviser. With complete disregard for his own safety Badcoe moved alone across 600 metres of fire-swept ground, attended to the wounded medical adviser and ensured his safety. He then organized a force of platoon strength and led them in a successful assault against the enemy machine-gun post near the body of the American adviser. He killed the machine-gunners in front of him, picked up the body of the dead American and ran back, over open ground still covered by hostile fire, to the regional force command post.

Two weeks later, early on 7 March 1967, the Sector Reaction Company was deployed to Quang Dien subsector to counter Viet Cong attack on the headquarters. Badcoe, who had left the command group when their vehicle broke down, joined the company headquarters and personally led the company in an attack over open terrain to capture a heavily defended enemy position. His action prevented the enemy from capturing the district headquarters and averted certain heavy losses.

Exactly one month later, on 7 April, Badcoe was on an operation with the 1st Army of the Republic of Vietnam Division Reaction Company, supported by armoured personnel carriers, in the Huong Tra district. As the 1st Army moved forward to its objective the company came under heavy small arms fire and had to withdraw to a nearby cemetery for cover. Badcoe and his radio operator were left fifty metres in front of the others, under heavy mortar fire. Badcoe ran back and rallied his men and got them moving but they were again stopped by heavy fire. He rose to throw grenades but was pulled down by his radio operator. When he got up to throw another grenade he was killed by a burst of machine-gun fire. Soon after friendly artillery was called in on the enemy position and it was assaulted and captured.

Badcoe was buried at the Terendak cemetery, Malaysia, his epitaph being 'He lived and died a soldier'. In November 1967 an Australian and New Zealand soldier's club in Vietnam was officially opened as the Peter Badcoe Club. A training block at the Officer Cadet School, Portsea, was also named Badcoe Hall in his honour.

For his services in Vietnam, in addition to the Victoria Cross, Badcoe was also awarded the American Silver Star. South Vietnam awarded him the National Order of the Republic of Vietnam (Knight), three Crosses of Gallantry (with Palm, Gold Star and Silver Star) and the Armed Forces Honour Medal, 1st Class.

Badcoe married Denise Maureen MacMahon on 26 May 1956. He had a family of three girls. His widow, who subsequently remarried, and his three daughters presented his medals to the Australian War Memorial for display in the Hall of Valour.

PAYNE Keith

RANK   Warrant Officer
Class II
UNIT   Australian Army
Training Team,
Vietnam
DATE   24 May 1969
PLACE   Kontum province,
South Vietnam (now
the Socialist Republic
of Vietnam)

KEITH PAYNE was born at Ingham, Queensland, on 30 August 1933, the son of Henry Thomas Payne. He was educated at Ingham state school and then apprenticed as a cabinetmaker. On 13 August 1951 he enlisted in the regular army, after a short period in the CMF, and was posted to the 1st Battalion, the Royal Australian Regiment in September 1952. He served in Korea with the 1st Battalion from April 1952 until March 1953, then the 28th British Commonwealth Infantry Brigade Defence and Employment Platoon, and returned to Queensland in September where he married Florence Catherine Plaw, of the WRAAC, on 5 December 1954.

Periods with the 4th Cadet and the 11th National Service Training Battalions followed, and on 17 February 1960 he joined the 3rd Battalion. He accompanied the 3rd to Malaya, was promoted to sergeant on 1 June 1961 and in February 1965 joined the 5th Battalion; promotion to temporary warrant officer class II came on 4 June 1965. The following June he went as company sergeant major to the Officer Training Unit and from February 1967 until March 1968 served in Papua New Guinea with the 2nd Pacific Islands Regiment. He was posted to Headquarters Northern Command at Brisbane prior to being appointed to the Training Team in Vietnam on 24 February 1969.

Payne soon joined a mobile strike force battalion which was reconnoitring enemy infiltration routes from Laos into Vietnam. Once the routes were located they were interdicted in an attempt to relieve the pressure on the recently constructed and occupied Ben Het Special Forces camp.

On 24 May (nearly two weeks after Ray Simpson [*see* following entry] won the Victoria Cross) Payne was commanding the 212th Company of the 1st Mobile Strike Force Battalion when the battalion was attacked by a numerically superior North Vietnamese force. The two forward companies were heavily attacked with rockets, mortars and machine-guns from three directions simultaneously. The indigenous soldiers faltered so Payne rushed about firing his Armalite rifle and hurling grenades to keep the enemy at bay while he tried to rally the soldiers. In doing so he was wounded in the hands, upper arm and hip by four pieces of rocket shrapnel and one piece of mortar shrapnel.

The battalion commander decided to fight his way back to base and this movement commenced by the only available route. With a few remnants of his company, which had suffered heavy casualties, Payne covered the withdrawal with grenades and gunfire and then attempted to round up more of his company. By nightfall he had succeeded in gathering a composite party of his own and another company and had established a small defensive perimeter, about 350 metres north-east of the hill. The enemy by now had captured the former hilltop position.

In darkness Payne set off to locate those who had been cut off and disoriented. At 9 p.m. he crawled over to one displaced group, having tracked them by the fluorescence of their footsteps in rotting vegetable matter on the ground, and thus began an 800 metre traverse of the area for the next three hours. The enemy were moving about and firing, but Payne was able to locate some forty men, some wounded, some of whom Payne personally dragged out. He organized others who were not wounded to crawl out on their stomachs with wounded on their backs.

Once he concentrated his party he navigated them back to the temporary perimeter only to find the position abandoned by troops who had moved back to the battalion base. Undeterred he led his party, as well as another group of wounded encountered en route, back to the battalion base where they arrived at about 3 a.m.

Evacuated from Vietnam for medical reasons in September 1969, Payne received a warm public welcome at Brisbane before entering an army hospital for treatment. On his recovery he was posted as an instructor at the Royal Military College, Duntroon, remaining until he joined the 42nd Battalion, the Royal Queensland Regiment, at Mackay, Queensland, on 20 December 1972. He had been presented with his Victoria Cross by the Queen aboard *Britannia*, at Brisbane, on 13 April 1970. The United States awarded him the Distinguished Service Cross and the Silver Star while the Republic of Vietnam honoured him with its Cross of Gallantry with bronze star.

Payne was honoured in other ways: his photograph and citation are displayed in the Hall of Heroes at the John F. Kennedy Center for Military Assistance, Fort Bragg, North Carolina; he was made a freeman of the city of Brisbane and the shire of Hinchinbrook; a park in the Brisbane suburb of Stafford, where he lived at the time of his decoration, was named Keith Payne Park in July 1971; and his portrait was painted for the Australian War Memorial by Stanley Bourne.

Payne left the Army on 31 March 1975. During 1975 and 1976, with the rank of captain, he fought with the army of the Sultan of Oman in the Dhofar war. Although the British army seconded officers and men for this campaign, Payne as an Australian had to go there in a private capacity. His family, whose home in 1983 was at North Mackay, consists of five sons.

SIMPSON Rayene Stewart

RANK	Warrant Officer Class II
UNIT	Australian Army Training Team, Vietnam
DATE	6 and 11 May 1969
PLACE	Kontum Province, South Vietnam (now the Socialist Republic of Vietnam)

RAY SIMPSON was born at Chippendale, New South Wales, on 16 February 1926, the son of R.W. Simpson. Educated at Carlingford and Dumaresque Island public schools, Taree, New South Wales, he joined the second AIF on 15 March 1944 and was sent to the 41st/2nd Infantry Battalion, a 'holding' unit for young soldiers under nineteen years. On the morning of 5 August 1944, Simpson had his first taste of action when he was part of a detachment sent to reinforce the garrison troops at Cowra after the escape of several hundred Japanese prisoners-of-war. One of his duties that day was to man number one Vickers machine-gun, identical to number two gun which several hours earlier had been defended to the death by Privates Hardy and Jones who were both posthumously awarded the George Cross. He was first posted to the 2/3rd Pioneer Battalion, AIF and later served with an Advanced Ordnance Depot and the 26th Battalion, AIF.

Demobilized in January 1947, Simpson for four years worked at various jobs — tram conductor, builder's labourer, sugar canecutter, sailor around Papua New Guinea — before re-enlisting in 1951 for service in Korea with the 3rd Battalion, the Royal Australian Regiment. He was appointed lance corporal on 30 November 1951 and promoted to corporal on 21 January 1953. During this period he married Shoko Sakai, a Japanese citizen, on 5 March 1952.

He was posted to the 2nd Battalion in January 1954 and he served in Malaya with this unit for two years from October 1955. Simpson was next posted to 1st Special Air Service Company in November 1957 and served with that unit until selected as one of the initial group of advisers for the AATTV (Australian Army Training Team, Vietnam) who left by air for Vietnam in July 1962.

A year later he returned to the Special Air Service unit in Australia for twelve months' service before his second tour of duty with the AATTV in Vietnam commenced in July 1964. During this second tour he was awarded the Distinguished Conduct Medal for his actions when a patrol was ambushed at Tako on 16 September. Simpson, although severely wounded in the leg, held off the enemy while he called for assistance by radio. He and his men repelled several enemy assaults until help arrived, and none too soon as the ammunition had almost gone and Simpson was weak from loss of blood. He was evacuated by helicopter to the 6th Field Hospital at Nha Trang and he later convalesced at Tokyo.

Simpson had been promoted to sergeant on 1 July 1955 and to temporary warrant officer class II in July 1964, the latter promotion being confirmed on 1 October the same year.

On 16 May 1966 Simpson left the army for a second time but re-enlisted in Saigon a year later for his third period of service with the AATTV. When he performed the actions for which he was awarded the Victoria Cross he was serving in Kontum province, near the Laotian border, as commander of a mobile strike force.

In a battalion-scale operation on 6 May the 232nd Company of the Mobile Strike Force, under Simpson, was moving through a jungle of large trees and dense bamboo undergrowth in rain and poor visibility in II Corps area near the junction of the borders of Vietnam, Laos and Cambodia. When one of his platoons became heavily engaged with the enemy Simpson led the remainder of his company to its assistance. As the company moved forward, one of the platoon commanders, Australian Warrant Officer M.W. Gill, was seriously wounded and the assault began to falter. Simpson, in the face of heavy enemy fire, moved across open ground and carried Gill to safety. He returned to his company and then crawled forward to within ten metres of the enemy. From here he lobbed grenades into their positions. Simpson then ordered his company to withdraw and he and five indigenous soldiers covered the withdrawal.

Next morning Simpson's company rejoined the battalion in another position where it was resupplied. Three days later, on 10 May, contact was again made with the enemy, but insufficient air support and the reticence of the indigenous soldiers caused it to be broken off.

At first light the next day artillery pounded the enemy positions and the battalion moved forward again to find the bunkers unoccupied. The battalion probed ahead with Warrant Officer A.M. Kelly leading the 231st Company. In the first burst of fire from the next contact, Kelly was wounded and the battalion commander, Captain Green of the American Special Forces, was killed when he went to assist Kelly. Simpson quickly organized two platoons of soldiers and several advisers and led them to the location of the contact. Despite the fact that most of his soldiers had fled, Simpson moved forward through withering machine-gun fire in order to cover the initial evacuation of the casualties. The wounded, including Kelly, were evacuated but Simpson was unable to reach Green's body because of heavy, accurate enemy fire. He then covered the evacuation of the wounded to the helicopter pad by placing himself between them and the enemy. The action ended indecisively next day when the battalion was evacuated.

Simpson received his Victoria Cross from the Queen during an investiture held at Government House, Sydney, on 1 May 1970. The United States awarded him the Silver Star and the Bronze Star for Valour. In 1972 he took up a position as administrative officer at the Australian Embassy, Tokyo. He died of cancer in Tokyo on 18 October 1978 and was buried at the Yokohama war cemetery, Japan.

His medals and a portrait by Joshua Smith are displayed in the Hall of Valour at the Australian War Memorial and his photograph and citation are displayed in the Hall of Heroes, John F. Kennedy Center for Military Assistance, Fort Bragg, North Carolina, USA.

WHEATLEY Kevin Arthur

RANK	Warrant Officer Class II
UNIT	Australian Army Training Team, Vietnam
DATE	13 November 1965
PLACE	Tra Bong Valley, Quang Ngai province, South Vietnam (now the Socialist Republic of Vietnam)

'DASHER' WHEATLEY was born at Sydney on 13 March 1937. Educated at Maroubra Junction technical school, Sydney, he worked as a brick burner and machine operator prior to enlisting in the regular army in June 1956. He was posted to the 4th Battalion in September and then to the 3rd Battalion in March the following year; his first operational duty was with the 3rd Battalion in Malaya in 1957–59. In August 1959 he joined the 2nd Battalion and in

June 1961 transferred to the 1st Battalion. He joined the Training Team on 16 March 1965 as a temporary warrant officer; he had been appointed lance corporal on 19 January 1959, promoted to corporal 2 February 1959, and to sergeant 1 January 1964.

Arriving in Vietnam in early 1965 he spent six months with a Vietnamese battalion in Quang Tri province prior to being posted to Tra Bong with five other Australian warrant officers in October 1965 to relieve the previous group of advisers. From the Special Forces outpost deep in the enemy- dominated Tra Bong valley, in Quang Ngai province, the AATTV and American advisers conducted 'search and destroy' operations. The advisers, housed in an isolated area to which access was gained by Caribou aircraft operating from a small nearby strip, were attached to a Civil Irregular Defence Group (CIDG) of Vietnamese and Montagnard soldiers.

Daily patrols were conducted from the base to a design which gradually moved the probes further outwards. It was on one of these patrols, on 13 November 1965, that Wheatley performed the actions for which he was awarded the Victoria Cross. The company patrol had split into three platoon groups and Wheatley and Warrant Officer II R.J. Swanton were with the right-hand group. At about 1.40 p.m. Wheatley reported contact with Viet Cong soldiers and soon after he requested assistance. Captain Fazekas, who was with the centre platoon, organized about fifteen irregulars and

fought towards the scene of the action. He received another message from Wheatley to say that Swanton had been hit in the chest. Wheatley requested an air strike and an aircraft for casualty evacuation.

About this time the night platoon began to scatter and although the CIDG medical assistant told Wheatley that Swanton was dying, Wheatley refused to abandon him. He discarded his radio and half dragged, half carried Swanton, under heavy enemy small arms fire, out of the open rice paddies into a wooded area 200 metres away. A CIDG member, Private Dinh Do, who was assisting Wheatley, urged him to leave Swanton. Wheatley refused, and was seen to pull the pins from two grenades. Holding a grenade in each hand, he calmly awaited the encircling Viet Cong.

Captain Fazekas led the search party that found the two bodies next morning; both had died of gunshot wounds. (Fazekas was awarded the Military Cross for his courage in trying to relieve Wheatley and Swanton.)

Wheatley had married on 20 July 1954, and was survived by his wife Edna and four children. His body was returned to Australia for burial at Pine Grove Memorial Park, Blacktown, New South Wales. His name is commemorated in the New South Wales Garden of Remembrance at Rookwood war cemetery. In 1967 a trophy for annual competition between the Australian Services Rugby Union and the Sydney Rugby Football Union was inaugurated in his name. A sports arena at

Vung Tau, Vietnam, was named after him and his citation and photograph are displayed in the Hall of Heroes, John F. Kennedy Center for Military Assistance, Fort Bragg, North Carolina, USA. The United States also awarded him the Silver Star. He was made a Knight of the National Order of the Republic of Vietnam, and received the Military Merit Medal and the Cross of Gallantry with Palm.

APPENDIX I: VICTORIA CROSS WINNERS WHO WERE BORN IN OR WHO DIED IN AUSTRALIA BUT DID NOT SERVE WITH AUSTRALIAN UNITS

BELL Mark Sever

RANK	Lieutenant (later Colonel)
UNIT	Corps of Royal Engineers
BORN	Sydney, NSW, 15 May 1843
DIED	Windlesham, Surrey, 26 June 1906
VC	Ordashsu, Ghana (Ashanti war), 4 February 1874

CALDWELL Thomas

RANK	Sergeant
UNIT	12th Battalion, The Royal Scots Fusiliers
BORN	Carluke, Lanarkshire, Scotland, 10 February 1894
DIED	Adelaide, SA, 6 June 1969
VC	Near Audenarde, Belgium, 31 October 1918

EVANS Arthur (alias SIMPSON, Walter)

RANK	Lance sergeant
UNIT	6th Battalion, The Lincolnshire Regiment
BORN	Everton, Liverpool, Lancashire, UK, 8 April 1891
DIED	Sydney, NSW, 31 October 1936
VC	South-west of Etaing, France, 2 September 1918

GEE Robert

RANK	Temporary captain
UNIT	2nd Battalion, The Royal Fusiliers
BORN	Leicester, UK, 7 May 1876
DIED	Perth, WA, 2 August 1960
VC	Masnières and Les Rues Vertes, France, 30 November 1917

GORMAN James

RANK	Seaman Unit Royal Navy (Naval Brigade)
BORN	1835(?)
DIED	Spectacle Island, Parramatta River, NSW, 18 October 1882

VC	Battle of Inkerman, Crimea, 5 November 1854

GRADY Thomas

RANK	Private Unit 4th Regiment (now The King's Own [Royal Border] Regiment)
BORN	Cheddah, Galway, Ireland, 18 September 1835
DIED	South Melbourne, Vic, 18 May 1891
VC	Crimea, 18 October and 22 November 1854

HEAPHY Charles

RANK	Major
UNIT	Auckland Militia, New Zealand Military Forces
BORN	St John's Wood, London, UK, 1822
DIED	Toowong, Qld, 3 August 1881
VC	New Zealand, 11 February 1864

HEATHCOTE Alfred Spencer

RANK	Lieutenant
UNIT	2nd Battalion, 60th Rifles (later The Royal Green Jackets)
BORN	London, 29 March 1832
DIED	Bowral, NSW, 21 February 1912
VC	Indian mutiny, June–September 1857

HOLLAND John Vincent

RANK	Lieutenant
UNIT	7th Battalion, Leinster Regiment

BORN	Athy, County Kildare, Ireland, 19 July 1889
DIED	Hobart, Tas, 27 February 1975
VC	Guillemont, France, 3 September 1916

HOLMES Frederick William

RANK	Lance corporal Unit 2nd Battalion, The King's Own Yorkshire Light Infantry
BORN	Tottenham, Middlesex, UK, 13 September 1889
DIED	Port Augusta, SA, 22 October 1969
VC	Le Cateau, France, 26 August 1914

MAGNER Michael (alias BARRY)

RANK	Drummer
UNIT	1st Battalion, 33rd Regiment (later The Duke of Wellington's [West Riding] Regiment)
BORN	Fermanagh, Ireland, 21 June 1840
DIED	Fitzroy, Vic, 6 February 1897
VC	Abyssinia, 13 April 1868

MOOR George Raymond Dallas

RANK	Second lieutenant
UNIT	3rd Battalion, The Hampshire Regiment
BORN	St Kilda, Vic, 22 October 1896
DIED	Mouveaux, France, 3 November 1918
VC	South of Krithia, Gallipoli, 5 June 1915

NAPIER William

RANK	Sergeant
UNIT	1st Battalion, 13th Regiment (now The Light Infantry)
BORN	Bingley, Yorkshire, UK, 1828
DIED	Rochester, Victoria, 2 June 1908
VC	Indian mutiny, 6 April 1858

O'HEA Timothy

RANK	Private
UNIT	1st Battalion, The Rifle Brigade (Prince Consort's Own)
BORN	Skull, Bantry, County Cork, Ireland, 1846
DIED	Sturt's Desert, Qld, November 1874
VC	Danville railway station, Quebec, Canada, 9 June 1866 (peacetime award)

PATON John

RANK	Sergeant
UNIT	2nd Battalion, 93rd Regiment (later The Argyll and Sutherland Highlanders — Princess Louise's)
BORN	Stirling, Scotland, 23 December 1833
DIED	Sydney, NSW, 1 April 1914
VC	Indian mutiny, 16 November 1857

SMITH Issy

RANK	Acting Corporal
UNIT	1st Battalion, Manchester Regiment
BORN	East London, UK, 16 September 1886
DIED	Melbourne, Vic, 11 September 1940
VC	St Julien, Belgium, 26 April 1915

SMYTH Maskylyne (later Sir Nevill)

RANK	Captain (later Major General)
UNIT	2nd Dragoon Guards
BORN	Westminster, London, UK, 14 August 1868
DIED	Balmoral, Vic, 18 July 1941
VC	Battle of Khartoum, Sudan, 2 September 1898

STANNARD Richard Been

RANK	Lieutenant
UNIT	Royal Naval Reserve
BORN	Blyth, Northumberland, UK, 21 August 1902
DIED	Sydney, NSW, 22 July 1977
VC	HMS *Arab*, Namsos, Norway, 28 April – 2 May 1940

WHIRLPOOL Frederick (born CONKER, alias JAMES, Frederick Humphrey)

RANK	Private
UNIT	3rd Bombay European Regiment (later The Prince of Wales Leinster Regiment)
BORN	Liverpool, UK, 1829
DIED	Near Windsor, NSW, 24 June 1899
VC	Indian mutiny, 3 April and 2 May 1858

APPENDIX II: THE GEORGE CROSS

ON 23 September 1940, almost a year after the outbreak of war, King George VI announced the creation of a new honour for civilians of both sexes — the George Cross and the George Medal. (The original warrant of this date was later cancelled and replaced by one of 8 May 1941.)

The George Cross is awarded 'only for acts of the greatest heroism of the most conspicuous courage in circumstances of extreme danger'. Although intended primarily for civilians throughout the Commonwealth, members of the armed services are eligible to receive it. Posthumous awards are made, recipients are entitled to the use of the post-nominals 'GC' after their names, and there is provision for the award of bars for further acts of heroism.

The decoration consists of a plain silver cross with a circular medallion in the centre, bearing a representation of St George and the Dragon, surrounded by the words 'For Gallantry'. In the angle of each arm of the cross is the Royal cypher 'GVI'. The reverse is plain and contains only the name of the recipient and the date of the award. The cross is suspended by a link from a silver bar adorned with a laurel leaf design, and the ribbon is dark blue, 3.75 cm wide. Women wear the cross on the left shoulder from a ribbon of the same width and colour, which is tied in a bow. When the ribbon is worn alone on undress uniform, a tiny silver replica is centered upon it, and the award of bars is indicated by the appropriate number of these small replicas.

Since its inception fourteen Australians have been awarded the George Cross. They are listed below.

Winners of the Medal of the Order of the British Empire for Gallantry (EGM) prior to 1940, who were still living, were able to exchange their medals for the George Cross. One Australian, Sir Gordon Taylor, who saved the monoplane *Southern Cross* piloted by Sir Charles Kingsford-Smith from disaster during an attempted crossing of the Tasman in May 1935, forfeited his EGM and received the new decoration in substitution.

Frederick Hamilton March, who won an Empire Gallentry Medal, and later exchanged it for the George Cross, was Australian-born. On 19 November 1924 he was acting as chauffeur to Sir Lee Stack,

Governor-General of the Sudan and Sirdar of the Egyptian Army, in Cairo, when seven Egyptians opened fire on the car from the pavement. Stack, his ADC and March were all wounded and had it not been for March's gallantry and presence of mind his passengers would almost certainly have been killed outright. Sir Lee Stack died next day from his wounds but March and the ADC survived. March died in relative obscurity in the Sudan.

Until 1940, however, when the George Cross was instituted, the Albert Medal was the highest award for civilian bravery. Since 1949 the Albert Medal has only been awarded posthumously. In 1971, the British government accepted the claim that surviving holders of the Albert and Edward Medals did not receive the recognition which was their undoubted due because of the decline in the significance and status of these awards. As a result all living holders of these medals were asked to exchange their awards for the George Cross. The Albert and Edward Medals, instituted in 1866 and 1907 respectively, ceased to be awarded from 1971 and their holders were henceforth entitled to use the post-nominals 'GC' and were invited to attend an investiture ceremony at Buckingham Palace to receive their George Crosses.

At that time six Australian holders of the Albert Medal were still alive and five of these accepted the investiture invitation. In all, twenty-five Australians had received the Albert Medal since 1887 when the first award was made in this country to William Yaldwyn who rescued six persons from a flood at Charleville, Queensland, in July 1886. The last awards were made posthumously in 1965 to Electrical Mechanic 1st Class William Condon and Midshipman Kerry Marien for gallantry at the sinking of HMAS *Voyager* on 10 February 1964. Eight Australians had received the Edward Medal but none were still living when the awards were exchanged.

George Cross Winners

BAILEY Eric George
RANK Sergeant
UNIT New South Wales Police Force
GC Blayney, NSW, 12 January 1945
London Gazette: 29 October 1946
BORN Tenterfield, NSW, 1906
DIED 12 January 1945

DONOGHUE Raymond Tasman
Tram conductor, Metropolitan Transport Trust, Tasmania
GC Hobart, 29 April 1960
BORN 1920
DIED 29 April 1960

EMANUEL Errol John
District Commissioner, East New Britain district, Territory of Papua New Guinea
GC East New Britain, July 1969 – 19 August 1971
BORN Enfield, NSW, 1918
DIED 19 August 1971

GOLDSWORTHY Leon Verdi
RANK Lieutenant Commander
UNIT Royal Australian Naval Volunteer Reserve (attached HMS *Vernon*)
GC Mine disposal, 12 June 1943 – 10 April 1944
London Gazette: 19 September 1944

BORN Broken Hill, NSW, 1909
Residing South Perth, WA

GOSSE George
RANK Lieutenant
UNIT Royal Australian Naval Volunteer Reserve (attached Royal Navy)
GC Mine recovery and disposal, 8–19 May 1945
London Gazette: 30 April 1946
BORN Harvey, WA, 1912
DIED 31 December 1964

HARDY Benjamin Glover
RANK Private
UNIT 22nd Australian Garrison Battalion, AMF
GC No. 12 Prisoner-of-War Camp, Cowra, 4–5 August 1944
BORN Marrickville, NSW, 1898
DIED 5 August 1944

JONES Ralph
RANK Private
UNIT 22nd Australian Garrison Battalion, AMF
GC No. 12 Prisoner-of-War Camp, Cowra, 4–5 August 1944
BORN Gorleston, Norfolk, UK, 1900
DIED 5 August 1944

MADDEN Horace William
RANK Private
UNIT 3rd Battalion, the Royal

Australian Regiment

GC — Prisoner-of-war, Korea, 24 April – 6 November 1951

BORN — Cronulla, NSW, 1924

DIED — 6 November 1951

MATTHEWS Lionel Colin

RANK — Captain

UNIT — 8th Division, AIF, Signals

GC — Prisoner-of-war, Sandakan, Borneo, August 1942 – March 1944

BORN — Stepney, SA, 1912

DIED — 2 March 1944

MOULD John Stuart

RANK — Lieutenant

UNIT — Royal Australian Naval Volunteer Reserve (attached HMS *Vernon*)

GC — Mine disposal, March 1941 – November 1942 *London Gazette*: 3 November 1942

BORN — Gosforth, Newcastle-on-Tyne, UK, 1910

DIED — 9 August 1957

PRATT Michael Kenneth

RANK — Constable Victoria Police Force

GC — Clifton Hill, Melbourne, 4 June 1976

BORN — East Melbourne, Vic, 1954 Residing Greensborough, Vic

ROGERS Jonathan

RANK — Chief Petty Officer (Coxswain)

UNIT — HMAS *Voyager*, Royal Australian Navy

GC — *Voyager/Melbourne* disaster, 10 February 1964

BORN — Llangollen, Denbighshire, UK, 1920

DIED — 10 February 1964

SYME Hugh Randall

RANK — Lieutenant

UNIT — Royal Australian Naval Volunteer Reserve (attached HMS *Vernon*)

GC — Mine recovery and disposal, 19 May 1941 – 25 December 1942 *London Gazette*: 3 August 1943

BORN — Melbourne, Vic, 1903

DIED — 7 November 1965

TAYLOR George Anthony Morgan

Vulcanologist, Commonwealth Bureau of Mineral Resources, Territory of Papua and New Guinea

GC — Mount Lamington, Papua, January 1951

BORN — Moree, NSW, 1917

DIED — 19 August 1972

Albert Medallists who exchanged their awards for the George Cross

BAGOT Arthur Gerald, DSC

RANK	Lieutenant
UNIT	Royal Naval Volunteer Reserve
DATE	12 April 1918 (explosion on motor launch)
LONDON GAZETTE	20 August 1918

CHALMERS Jack

DATE	4 February 1922 (shark attack)
PLACE	Coogee Beach, Sydney, NSW
LONDON GAZETTE	7 July 1922

GIBBS Stanley F.

DATE	3 January 1927 (shark attack)
PLACE	Port Hacking, Sydney, NSW
LONDON GAZETTE	8 February 1927

KAVANAUGH Robert Murray

DATE	12 January 1929 (shark attack)
PLACE	Bondi Beach, Sydney, NSW
LONDON GAZETTE	17 October 1930

McALONEY William Simpson

RANK	Aircraftman
DATE	31 August 1937 (rescue from burning aircraft)
PLACE	Hamilton, Vic
LONDON GAZETTE	18 February 1938

RICHARDS Richard Walter

DATE	Shackleton Trans-Antarctic Expedition, 1915
PLACE	Ross Sea, Antarctica
LONDON GAZETTE	5 July 1923

INDEX OF VICTORIA CROSS WINNERS

AUSTRALIAN WAR MEMORIAL
PHOTOGRAPHIC RECORD FILE NUMBERS

Anderson C.G.W.	100636	Edwards H.I.	42687/A
Axford T.L.	J3060		
		French J.A.	100643
Badcoe P.J.	116857		
Beatham R.	J3073	Gaby A.E.	A2622
Bell F.W.	A3687	Gordon B.S.	A3693
Bidsee J.H.	A3685/B	Gordon J.H.	Z1197
Birks F.	A3690	Gratwick P.E.	100640
Blackburn A.	J3069/A	Grieve R.C.	H38
Borella A.	H3331	Gurney A.S.	100639A
Brown W.E.	A2600		
Buckley A.	H6648	Hall A.C.	H12525
Buckley M.V.	A5136	Hamilton J.	J3071
Bugden P.J.	H12601	Howell G.J.	J3080/A
Burton A.	H6785	Howse N.R.	A1189
Carrol J.	D15	Ingram G.M.	J3067
Cartwright G.	J3063/A	Inwood R.R.	H6193
Castleton C.	H6769		
Cherry P.H.	H6507	Jacka A.	A2868
Chowne A.	134484/A	Jackson J.W.	A2641
Cooke T.	A2649	Jeffries C.S.	H12594
Currey W.	J3065/A	Jensen J.C.	H6203a
Cutler A.R.	13490S	Joynt W.D.	A3534
Dalziel H.	H15992	Kenna E.	134485/A
Dartnell W.T.	A1585	Kenny T.J.	D14
Davey P.	D67	Kelliher R.	131284
Derrick T.C.	141308	Keysor L.M.	D21
Dunstan W.	H6201	Kibby W.H.	61363
Dwyer J.J.	E1731/A	Kingsbury B.S.	100112
Edmondson J.H.	100642	Leak J.	H6716

Lowerson A.D.	A2650	Rattey R.R.	134906/A
		Rogers J.	42688A
Mackey J.B.	134468/A	Ruthven W.	D19
Mactier R.	H67	Ryan J.	A2621/A
Maygar L.C.	H12606		
Maxwell J.	P171/02/02	Sadlier C.W.K.	D22
McCarthy L.D.	H13822	Shout A.J.	G1028
McDougall S.R.	A5155	Simpson R.S.	106076
McGee L.	A2623	Starcevich L.T.	124956/A
McNamara F.H.	P336/01/01	Statton P.C.	H3332
Middleton R.H.	100641	Storkey P.V.	A4827
Moon R.V.	A2592	Symons W.J.	H6206
Murray H.W.	H9	Sullivan A.P.	A2497
Newland J.E.	A2614	Throssell H.V.H.	A3688
Newton W.E.	106584	Towner E.T.	J3070
		Tubb F.H.	H6786
O'Meara M.	H12763		
		Wark B.A.	A5435
Partridge F.J.	131225/A	Weathers L.C.	H6789
Payne K.	LES/69/593/UN	Wheatley K.A.	81392
Pearse S.G.	H6653	Whittle J.W.	H6186
Peeler W.	D16	Woods J.P.	A2640
Pope C.	A2648	Wylly G.G.	A4423

AUSTRALIANS
AWARDED
THE
VICTORIA CROSS